NOLO *and* **USA TODAY**

 ## **NOLO**
YOUR LEGAL COMPANION

For more than 35 years, Nolo has been helping ordinary folks who want to answer their legal questions, create their own documents, or work with a lawyer more efficiently. Nolo.com provides quick information about wills, house buying, credit repair, starting a business—and just about anything else that's affected by the law. It's packed with free articles, legal updates, resources, and a complete catalog of Nolo books and software.

To find out about any important legal changes to this book's contents, check for free updates at Nolo.com. Under "Products," find this book and click "Legal Updates." You can also sign up for our free e-newsletters at Nolo.com/newsletters/index.html.

 ## **USA TODAY**
The Nation's Newspaper

USA TODAY, the nation's largest circulation newspaper, was founded in 1982. It has nearly 3.9 million readers daily, making it the most widely read newspaper in the country.

USATODAY.com adds blogs, interactive graphics, games, travel resources, and trailblazing network journalism, allowing readers to comment on every story.

Nannies & Au Pairs

Hiring In-Home Child Care

Ilona Bray, J.D.

First Edition	MAY 2010
Editor	JANET PORTMAN
Cover Design	SUSAN PUTNEY
Book Design	SUSAN PUTNEY
Proofreading	SUSAN CARLSON GREENE
Index	SONGBIRD INDEXING SERVICES
Printing	DELTA PRINTING SOLUTIONS, INC.

Bray, Ilona, 1962-
  Nannies and au pairs : hiring in-home child care / by Ilona Bray. -- 1st ed.
    p. cm.
  ISBN-13: 978-1-4133-1190-7 (pbk.)
  ISBN-10: 1-4133-1190-3 (pbk.)
  1. Child care services--United States. 2. Nannies--United States. 3. Au pairs--United
States. I. Title.
  HQ778.7.U6B72 2010
  649'.1--dc22
                                        2009046881

Acknowledgments

A number of parents and experienced nannies and au pairs across the United States—in fact, around the world—were kind enough to share stories and ideas for this book. They include: Jennifer Castner, Vivian Chern, Lise Dahms, Jack Devaney, Christine Farley, Diana Fitzpatrick, Amy Hevly, Susan Messina, Shylah Robinson, Marcia Stewart, Jackie Thompson, and others.

Various professionals also provided valuable information on financial and other industry matters, including Tom Breedlove of Breedlove and Associates (www.breedlove-online.com); Bob King, attorney and founder of Legally Nanny, in Irvine, California (www.legallynanny.com); Mike Mansel of Argo Insurance in California (www.argoinsurance.com and www.publiability.com); Helene Young of USAuPair in Lake Oswego, Oregon (www.usaupair.com); and Stacey Frank, of Agent Au Pair in San Francisco (http://agentaupair.com).

Here at Nolo, attorney Lisa Guerin contributed insights on employment policies and legal matters. Janet Portman brought both legal acumen and personal experience to the task of editing. And thanks, finally, to Nolo's Production Department, including Jaleh Doane, Susan Putney, and Ashley Garst.

About the Author

Ilona Bray is an author and legal editor at Nolo, specializing in real estate, immigration law, and nonprofit fundraising. Among the many books she has authored are *Healthy Employees, Healthy Business: Easy, Affordable Ways to Promote Workplace Wellness, Effective Fundraising for Nonprofits,* and *Nolo's Essential Guide to Buying Your First Home* (as coauthor).

Long before Ms. Bray began writing books for Nolo, her first paid jobs involved reading books to children—that is, doing babysitting and child care jobs, the starting point for many working women. She later received her law degree and a Masters degree in East Asian (Chinese) studies from the University of Washington. Her background as a lawyer includes solo practice, nonprofit, and corporate stints, as well as long periods of volunteering.

Table of Contents

Your Companion When Hiring a Nanny or an Au Pair

Being a parent puts you into many new roles. Suddenly you're expected to be your child's nurse, tutor, games coordinator, costume designer, psychologist, and of course sleep coach. But when it's time for you to step back into the workplace, you may want to add yet another role to your already-impressive list: that of an employer to an in-home nanny or au pair.

If you're like most parents, you'd rather change 1,000 diapers than deal with some of the tasks involved in hiring a nanny. These tasks can include everything from advertising to dealing with tax and payroll issues to supervising and perhaps even firing a nanny. All of this is set against a potentially stress-inducing background, in which your decisions have consequences for your child's health, development, and safety.

That's where this book comes in. We'll show you how to make some difficult tasks easy and tell you when others are sufficiently complicated that you should save yourself the effort and hand them over to a professional.

We'll take the process step-by-step, covering issues like:

- deciding whether a nanny, an au pair, or some other form of child care fits your needs and budget best
- finding, interviewing, and screening a nanny or an au pair
- understanding how the immigration laws affect who you can legally hire
- dealing with payroll and tax requirements and taking advantage of tax credits
- training your new nanny or au pair

- developing an ongoing routine that you and your nanny or au pair are happy with, and

- ending the relationship, either when the time comes or because it's a bad match.

In the short time it takes you to read this book, you'll discover that there was more to know about hiring nannies and au pairs than you expected—but that most of it is fairly easy to understand and work with. We've tried to make it even easier for you, with handy checklists of things like interview questions and "to do" tasks, sample letters and agreements, and more. And with these tools, you'll be able to find a nanny or an au pair who will become a trusted, levelheaded presence in your household, and a friend as well as caregiver to your child. ●

Making the Choice: A Nanny or Another Form of Child Care?

You may be pretty sure that your Number One choice for child care is hiring a nanny—someone who comes to your home (or even lives there) to take personal care of your children. But you've probably heard that nannies are the most expensive form of child care, and that having someone in your home for substantial periods of time, let alone living there, can be a challenge. Before deciding for certain that hiring a nanny is the best type of child care for you, read quickly through this chapter to learn the ups and downs of this set-up, as told by many who have firsthand experience. Take a look at other child care options, too; and examine your finances to make sure that you can afford hiring a nanny. This chapter will show you the big picture by explaining:

- the range of child care options and their general advantages and disadvantages
- the comparative costs of a nanny and other forms of child care
- how much of your time or money you can put toward child care, and
- ways to save money by supplementing nanny care, such as with regular play dates or child care trades for children.

Even if you feel absolutely sure you want to hire a nanny, keep reading. You'll pick up some important tips on figuring out how much you can spend and how to bring the costs down.

TIP

How soon will you need the nanny? If you'll need someone within the next few weeks, start moving quickly. Advertising for, preparing for, and lining up the right nanny usually takes from four to eight weeks. But don't start earlier than that, because the nannies you'll find will probably want to begin work sooner than you're ready.

Beyond Mary Poppins: Child Care Options

Other than in-home nanny care, most parents also consider preschools, international au pairs (which we'll also cover in this book), and day care centers (whether in a school-type setting or in someone's home). Below is a summary of the advantages and disadvantages these options offer compared to nannies.

 TIP
A blend of child care set-ups might be best for your child.
Your choice of child care should take into account (among other things) your child's needs and temperament. For example, a very shy child might benefit from the socialization a large day care center provides—but not too much all at once. (Studies have shown that shy children in day care produce more stress hormones.) Combining a few hours a day at a day care center with other hours spent with a nanny might be the best arrangement.

Nannies

A nanny is someone who, if she's not invited to live with you, comes regularly to your home to provide individual care for your child (or children). Most nannies are women, though male nannies, sometimes called mannies, do exist. For simplicity's sake, we'll refer to both them throughout this book as "her" or "she."

Having a nanny allows your child to remain in a familiar setting, with favorite books, toys, and food nearby, on a schedule that fits your work or other needs. Instead of having to rush every morning to make sure your child is fed, dressed, and out the door on time, you can simply turn matters over to the nanny.

Ideally, the nanny and your child will build a close, caring relationship. A nanny can start to feel almost like part of the family. This doesn't mean your child will be stuck at home with no one but the nanny for company, however. A good nanny will take your child out to the zoo, the park, play dates with other children, and story time at the library.

Tips for Parents Working at Home

According to Susan in Washington, DC, who works with parents, "I frequently encounter a couple of misconceptions among expectant parents who plan to work at home after the baby arrives.

"The first one is, 'I can take care of the baby at the same time I do my job.' Unless you have a baby who sleeps constantly, that simply won't work.

"Then the parents say, 'I'll hire a nanny and she'll take care of the baby, but I'll be around to watch over things,' and I say, 'That can be totally great and that's what I did, but make sure you have a dedicated workspace.'

"If, for example, you have a studio apartment, and you're planning to be in one corner, with the nanny and baby in another, it's not going to work. Your child is going to demand your attention—and even if not, you may not be able to resist crossing the room yourself.

"With a separate room where you can close the door, a child under the age of about 18 months or two years will literally not realize you're nearby. You're out of sight, out of mind, and the nanny can capture the child's full attention.

"After a child reaches that transition age, of course, sharing space gets trickier. I encouraged my daughter's nannies to spend a lot of time out of the house, going to the park, or the library, or socializing with other nannies—they've typically got a whole network to tap into. But if it was a cold rainy day, or my daughter was sick, the day would be excruciating. I could hear her wailing and wanting me, while I was, say, stuck on a conference call. Luckily, those days were few and far between, or I might have had to rethink the whole plan."

> **TIP**
> **"We bought a zoo pass our nanny could use."** Dalia, the mother of two boys in Piedmont, California, explains: "That way, we made sure there was at least one interesting place the nanny could regularly take the boys without worrying about added expense. We also soon found that she was part of a network of other Laotian nannies, all of whom met regularly with the children at a nearby lake."

Some nannies are additionally willing to perform light household chores, particularly those relating to your child. This might include doing the child's laundry, preparing the child's lunch and snacks, tidying up, and more. Of course, as we'll discuss in Chapter 9, all of this should be negotiated in advance.

The attractive aspects of having a nanny come with a price. Nannies are by far the most expensive type of child care, typically costing at least $18,000 a year for full-time care—and that's before you start figuring in bonuses, eventual raises, and reimbursement for incidentals. (Such incidentals might include, for example, her lunch when she takes the kids out, and the costs of gas when ferrying your children around, or even for the nanny's commute, which some parents pay for.)

USA TODAY Snapshots®

Who's minding the tots?
Regular primary child-care arrangements for 2-year-olds, 2003-04:

No non-parental care — 50%
Relative — 19%
Center-based — 16%
Non-relative — 15%
Multiple[1] — 1%

1 – Multiple arrangements are when an equal amount of time is spent in two or more arrangements. Percentages do not add up to 100% Because of rounding.

Source: U.S. Department of Education

By Tracey Wong Briggs and Frank Pompa, USA TODAY 2006

What's more, the payment system itself is complex. Because you'll be considered the nanny's employer, you'll have to pay Social Security and other taxes (discussed in Chapter 5). You may find yourself hiring an accountant or tax preparer for the first time. The exception, of course, is to pay a nanny under the table. Unfortunately, that's not only illegal, but you'd lose the various tax deductions available in connection with child care expenses—and if the nanny happens also to be an undocumented alien, you risk her being deported on short notice. We'll discuss the risks and realities of paying under the table in Chapter 5.

> **TIP**
> **The more children you have, the more cost-effective a nanny gets.** Unlike day care centers, a nanny doesn't double or triple her salary when you add another child into the mix (though it will go up some). In other words, using a nanny becomes cost-effective when she'll be caring for more than one child. So, if you've just had triplets, start reading the nanny ads!

Another disadvantage to nannies is the amount of unsupervised control they have over your child and home. Although this book will help you make sure you get an excellent nanny, the state doesn't help you out with any licensing procedures, and taking that initial leap of trust can be unnerving. Cases of nannies committing child abuse, theft, or other crimes are infrequent, but they do occur. Less drastically, if the nanny gets sick or doesn't show up for any reason, you may be scrambling to find alternate care that day. In fact, as you look for a nanny, it's also worth collecting names of possible backup nannies.

> **CAUTION**
> **Not every nanny is a professional nanny.** As International Nanny Association President Pat Cascio told USA TODAY, "Professional nannies are career child care providers, generally women ages 21 to 50. They usually are college educated, often with degrees in early childhood development or education. The majority are trained in CPR and first aid; some are former pediatric nurses. Nannies work 40 to 70 hours a week on a live-in or live-out basis. The annual salary ranges from $22,000 to $60,000, depending on experience and location. Benefits often include insurance, paid vacation, and room and board."

Nannies Who Live In

Hiring a live-in nanny, instead of one who comes to your home for specified hours only, adds a whole new set of advantages and disadvantages to the mix described above. Convenience and flexibility are among the main advantages. You'll never have to worry about your nanny missing the bus or getting stuck in traffic. Although you can't expect her to work around the clock, arranging that she do some night hours, or trading a couple of hours on one day for extra babysitting on another should be fairly simple. All of this comes at a price that's less than you'd pay a nanny who does not live in. That's a surprise to many parents, but it is, in fact, traditional to lower the salary in light of the fact that you're providing room and board. However, you wouldn't go so far as to subtract the exact amount that a local rental unit would cost. We'll talk more about setting a salary in Chapter 4.

Not everyone has the space available for a live-in arrangement, however. Ideally, you'd want to offer not only a separate bedroom, but a separate bathroom, too. Even if you can offer both, there's no question that you'll be giving up some privacy and sense of family intimacy. Your nanny will see you at your best and worst and during hours of the day when you'd rather not talk to anyone, period. Jackie, a single mom living in the New York City metro area, says, "At the end of a tough week, I'd just want some time alone with my son—not to mention the fact that when the nanny was always around, I never got to be the 'fun' one, but was always the disciplinarian and the one who put him to bed. One way I dealt with this was to give the nanny free movie tickets and the use of my car, just to get her out of the house!"

Unlike the nanny who goes home after her shift, your live-in nanny won't have the ability to leave work behind when her hours are done. If the day or evening has produced stress or the job starts to wear on her, or other personal issues come up, you may have to deal with the consequences.

Vivian, from Princeton, New Jersey, says, "We wouldn't have had live-ins if we'd had a choice. We finished the basement so our nanny would have her own space downstairs. But we found with more than one of our nannies that, because she'd already built her life around our family, she'd want to hang out, eat dinner, and enjoy our company even when she wasn't working. I was a medical resident when my first son was born, and was often on call, so I couldn't come home from working 36 hours and start taking care of everyone."

Questions about who interacts with and disciplines the child get more complex when a full-time nanny and the parent(s) are on the scene all the time. At dinnertime, for example, if your child has a tantrum and demands different food, who steps in? (Does it matter whether it was you or the nanny who prepared the food?)

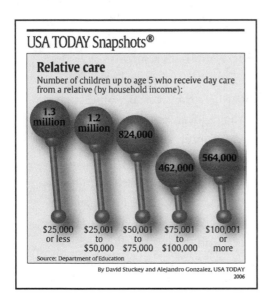

USA TODAY Snapshots®

Relative care
Number of children up to age 5 who receive day care from a relative (by household income):

1.3 million — $25,000 or less
1.2 million — $25,001 to $50,000
824,000 — $50,001 to $75,000
462,000 — $75,001 to $100,000
564,000 — $100,001 or more

Source: Department of Education
By David Stuckey and Alejandro Gonzalez, USA TODAY 2006

And you're bound to encounter some ego-deflating moments when, for example, you go to tuck your child in and he says, "Go away, Mom. I want my nanny." By the way, this is normal—all young kids have moments of playing favorites and feeling particularly strong affections toward different people in their lives, and they don't realize how harsh such statements sound. When it happens, just remember that things could be worse—you could have hired a nanny the child is scared of. Deep down, children know who their parents are.

Au Pairs

An au pair is a young person from another country, proficient in English, who has signed up with a cultural exchange program to both live with and provide child care for an American family. Because it's a formal program, subject to U.S. immigration laws, you have a lot less leeway to set hours and rules than you do with a regular nanny. We'll talk about this program in detail in Chapter 8.

Working Moms: Stop Feeling Guilty!

Vivian, a working mom and practicing psychiatrist in Princeton, New Jersey, offers this reassurance: "When you're a mother, you're a mother all the time—it doesn't matter if you're working. Some people will try to guilt you about things like missing out on your child's first word. But you can be a full-time mom and happen to be in the bathroom when that happens!"

The best reason to hire an au pair is that it's inexpensive. You pay a set amount, regardless how many children you have. You also pay various fees, but even after accounting for them, the cost works out to about $8 per hour.

If you like the idea of an energetic, educated young person living with you for a limited time at a low pay rate, this program might be for you. However, a common mistake made by host families is thinking they're getting a nanny who'll want just a few extracurricular activities on the side. They soon discover that all but the most homebody-ish of au pairs tend to expect lots of extracurricular activities with a little child care on the side.

Successful balances can be struck—most of the time. If, for example, you live in a remote location in a house with few amenities, and you end up with an au pair who was hoping for big-city excitement and weekend parties with fellow au pairs, don't be surprised if your au pair leaves early—or you have to ask her to leave.

> **CAUTION**
> **Many au pairs are still teenagers.** According to Kay, a parent in Berkeley, California, "We've loved all five of the au pairs that we've had, but definitely had to get used to some personal quirks. One au pair, for example, was wonderfully creative and enthusiastic with our child, but as surly as any teenager when talking with us. And as soon as they're off work, they're usually either meeting up with friends or catching up with them via cell phone or the Internet."

Licensed Day Care Centers

If you enroll your child in a licensed day care operation, you and a herd of other busy parents will drop your children off daily (or as otherwise arranged) at a small school-like location. The schedule is usually fairly strict, for a set period of hours each day. (Beware of late pickup fees!) Getting there by, say, 8:30 a.m. each day can be tough, but consider the flipside—a day care center can't call in sick like a nanny might. You can count on it being there every day.

Expect a structured environment, with trained teachers and carefully planned activities. The center should be clean and safe, in accordance with state guidelines and subject to state inspections.

> **RESOURCE**
> **Interested in your state's rules?** See the National Resource Center for Health and Safety in Child Care's website at http://nrc. uchsc.edu. The best day care centers also receive accreditation by the National Association for the Education of Young Children (NAEYC; www.naeyc.org).

A day care center can offer a lot of fun, stimulation, and social time for your children. Perhaps for you, too—some centers require or encourage parental involvement in field trips, fundraising, and more.

But day care centers can also mean less individual attention—not to mention more exposure to other kids' colds and illnesses. The average child under the age of three who's in day care picks up two illnesses a month. And if your child gets sick and needs to stay home, you'll have to find alternate care.

USA TODAY Snapshots®

Raising a child

What families will spend to raise a child born in 2008 through age 17[1]: Family income/Cost:

Less than $56,870 — $159,870
$56,870–$98,470 — $221,190
More than $98,470 — $366,660

1 – 2008 dollars
Source: USDA's Center for Nutrition Policy and Promotion

By Anne R. Carey and Alejandro Gonzalez, USA TODAY 2009

> ⚠ **CAUTION**
> **Many day care centers have an age minimum.** If you're looking for infant care, you may need to start with something else—perhaps a nanny. Or, the center may charge more for infants and young toddlers than for preschool age children.

In-Home Day Care Facilities

Day care centers that are run out of someone's home tend to operate less formally than their institutional cousins. While they require state licensing, this doesn't mean much—the oversight and enforcement tends to be lax. (Some home-based day care centers do, however, seek extra credentials in the form of accreditation from the National Association of Family Child Care (NAFCC; www.nafcc.org) which conducts an independent review that can take up to three years.

Some are staffed by only one person—perhaps a grandmother with an empty nest, or the new mother in the condo across the way who'd like to earn extra income while staying home with her baby. Nationwide, around 44% of in-home child care providers have only a high school diploma or less.

A highly regarded in-home child care facility with a loving, nurturing staff, offers some distinct advantages. Such facilities are, by law, supposed to take in fewer children per staff member than the more institutional day care centers. The location may feel more like home to a child. And because the structure is looser, you may be allowed more flexibility regarding when you pick up and drop off your child.

There are disadvantages to a small setting, however. The caregivers will likely have no relevant formal training, and the quality of such facilities varies widely, depending in part on the person's actual house and neighborhood. (You may encounter—and will probably quickly flee from—places where the kids are running around in the basement with the television on at top volume.) If the home is staffed by only one person, that person will have no supervision and no backup in case of illness or emergencies. As with institutional day care centers, exposure to more children means exposure to more germs.

Preschools

After your child has reached age three or so, preschool becomes an option. Similar to an institutional day care center, a preschool is a place where you deliver your child on a regular schedule, and he or she is cared for by trained, licensed staff members—in fact, teachers.

There's a reason they call it preschool. The goal is not merely to keep the child occupied while you're at work, but to help ready your child for "real" school. In keeping with that goal, you may find that the preschool hours are fewer than you need (for example, limited to a few mornings each week). You'll have to fill the gap with other forms of child care. You may also find that parental involvement, as well as financial donations or fundraising, are expected.

Considerations for a Special-Needs Child

If you have a child with special physical or mental needs, you'll of course want to take these into account when planning child care. Don't make the mistake of hiding your situation. First of all, federal law gives you some protection, making it illegal for child care centers and home-based day care centers to discriminate (by refusing your child entry or charging more) unless accommodating your child would require unreasonable expense. (The relevant law is called the Americans with Disabilities Act, or ADA.) Secondly, in order to give your child the best care, the provider needs to know the facts.

The ADA doesn't apply to nannies and other individual caregivers, however. They can refuse a job involving a special-needs child if they wish. As with a school or day care center or home, you'll need to be straightforward in explaining your child's needs—if for no other reason than to make sure the nanny has the strength and experience to provide adequate care. Be prepared to pay more than the local average for kids without special needs.

Budgeting for Child Care

In this section, we'll look first at how much a nanny or another form of child care costs and then at whether these costs fit within your household budget.

Child Care Costs

Here's a quick picture of the relative costs of different kinds of day care. The cost per child assumes enough hours to cover the time away from home of a full-time working parent.

Childcare Costs	
Type of day care	**Average monthly cost per child** (Excluding fees, extra charges, or overtime for special circumstances)
Nanny	$1,500 to $3,033
Au pair	$767 plus agency fees, certain living expenses, educational costs, and possibly airfare; cost remains the same regardless of the number of children
Day care center	$250 to $1,250
In-home day care	$281 to $860
Preschool	$338 to $973 (but probably for fewer hours than you need, thus requiring supplementation with other forms of care)

A nanny is clearly the most expensive option. But before you make any decisions based on nationwide averages, do some research about how much nannies actually cost in your area. The amount varies depending on location, supply and demand, a nanny's level of experience or relevant education (such as a childhood education degree), and your own household needs, including how many children you have and what tasks you expect the nanny to handle.

You may be surprised at what you learn about local nanny salaries— proof that it's important to do your homework. For example, parents in small towns often discover that they actually have to spend more for nannies than their friends in big cities, despite salaries for other jobs being low in their area. The lack of a large immigrant community is often the key variable, reducing the pool of available nannies in many small towns.

Ask other parents in your area for cost information and look at ads in local papers and online sources like Craigslist. Ultimately, you'll need to leave some room for negotiation with the nanny you'd like to hire, as discussed in Chapter 7.

The fact that nannies are expensive doesn't necessarily mean you should give up on hiring one. If your lifestyle really demands a nanny, the other options may turn out to be more expensive than they seem to be at first. For example, if your workday is long and you travel a lot (causing you to pay frequent late pickup fees at the day care center) and hire a lot of evening babysitters, a nanny's salary might start to look more reasonable.

TIP

You'll get tax breaks for child care expenses. We'll discuss how to take best advantage of the child care tax credit in Chapter 5. Also, ask your employer whether it offers a flexible spending plan (an FSA or "cafeteria plan"), in which you set aside part of your salary in pretax dollars to cover child care.

You're also likely to save money on doctor bills by hiring either a nanny or an au pair. Studies show that children in group day care centers are at two to four times higher risk of coming down with various infectious diseases compared with children cared for at home. Those copayments and missed days at work can add up—especially if your child is prone to picking up every passing germ or has immune system problems.

Now let's take a look at how much, in absolute terms, you can afford.

How Much Money Your Household Brings In

Before deciding whether you can afford a nanny, you'll need to get a handle on your household income. We recommend creating a worksheet like the Household Spending Plan below. Budgeting software (like *Quicken*, for example) or a spreadsheet like *Excel* can make this task easy. If you've already done this, you can skip ahead to the hiring section below.

Using a worksheet like the Household Spending Plan, below, enter your household's gross income (the amount before deductions like taxes, flexible spending accounts, and 401(k) withdrawals). Then, list those deductions. Doing so shows you where it's all going. You may want to make adjustments to some of those deductions, if necessary.

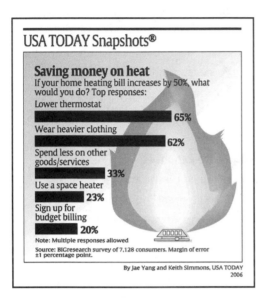

USA TODAY Snapshots®

Saving money on heat
If your home heating bill increases by 50%, what would you do? Top responses:

Lower thermostat
65%

Wear heavier clothing
62%

Spend less on other goods/services
33%

Use a space heater
23%

Sign up for budget billing
20%

Note: Multiple responses allowed
Source: BIGresearch survey of 7,128 consumers. Margin of error ±1 percentage point.

By Jae Yang and Keith Simmons, USA TODAY
2006

Your main source of income is most likely a paycheck or self-employment, so look at your pay stub or business records to find the net amount. But your income may also include tips, royalties, rental income, dividends, regular gifts from family, disability payments, child support, and so forth. If you pay taxes on these (such as dividends), take those taxes off the top.

How Much Money Is Going Out

To get a picture of your spending, fill in all your regular or predictable expenses on your Household Spending Plan, such as food, transportation, entertainment, rent or mortgage payments, other debt, and more. Look over your old receipts, credit card statements, and bank statements. Try to figure out averages, for example how much you spend each month on restaurant meals or clothes. (Some software programs will do this for you.) Don't forget any automatic monthly withdrawals, such as for your DSL line, DVD rental service, or gym membership.

Some of your most significant expenses may be yearly, such as your car or homeowners' insurance. Divide such yearly expenses by 12. Other expenses may occur weekly, irregularly, or as a single lump sum, so you'll need to play with the numbers to put them into monthly terms.

Regular bills and debt payments will be the easiest to figure out—but keep in mind that some will change over the course of the year, such as heating and cooling costs.

Cash spending can be the hardest to track. As Jean Chatzky, author of *Pay It Down! From Debt to Wealth on $10 a Day* told USA TODAY, "Most people pull out $100 or $200 from the ATM and lump it as 'cash,' but they don't know where it goes." Track your cash spending for a week or two and write it down.

Also include on your chart any regular deposits you already make into savings or retirement plans. And for your outstanding credit card balance, enter the minimum payment. (But recognize that you'll want to work toward paying this off before too long, to avoid high interest payments.)

Costs of children

Estimated average expenditures on a child from birth to age 18 by husband-and-wife families in the USA in 2005:

Total spent on raising a child

Low-income families
(less than $43,200 in pretax income)

$139,110

Middle-income families
($43,200 to $72,600 in pretax income)

$190,980

High-income familes
(more than $72,600 in pretax income)

$279,450

Source: Department of Agriculture

By Julie Snider, USA TODAY
2006

Household Spending Plan	
MONTHLY INCOME	
Household gross income	$
Federal tax withholding	−$
State tax withholding	−$
OASDI/Medicare/State SDI	−$
FSA Withholdings	−$
401(k)/403(b)/elective retirement withholding	−$
Disability insurance	−$
Household net income	$

MONTHLY EXPENSES	
Expense type	**Cost per month**
HOUSEHOLD EXPENSES	
Mortgage(s) (or rent)	$
Homeowners' association dues	$
Insurance (homeowners')	$
Property tax	$
Utilities	$
Water	$
Garbage	$
Gas	$
Sewer	$
Electric	$
Household furnishings	$
Household maintenance expenses	$
Appliances	$
Cleaning supplies	$
Maintenance supplies	$
Home office supplies (computer and printer, paper, file cabinets and folders, and postage stamps)	$

Household Spending Plan (cont'd)

MONTHLY EXPENSES (cont'd)

Expense type	Cost per month
HOUSEHOLD EXPENSES, cont'd	
Household services	$
Cleaning	$
Lawn and garden care	$
Other: (such as water heater or pool maintenance)	$
Phone and TV	$
Cell phone	$
Cable	$
Home phone/DSL	$
Other	$
Subtotal: Monthly household expenses	$
PERSONAL EXPENSES	
Groceries (not including meals out)	$
Health and dental expenses	$
Insurance (health, life, and other)	$
Prescriptions	$
Copays	$
Glasses	$
Clothing and shoes	$
Personal care (dry cleaning, haircuts, makeup, and massage)	$
Personal fitness and sports (gym membership, yoga classes, and children's activities and equipment)	$
Pets (food, walking, grooming, boarding services, and veterinary care)	$
Subtotal: Monthly personal expenses	$

Household Spending Plan (cont'd)	
MONTHLY EXPENSES (cont'd)	
Expense type	Cost per month
TRANSPORTATION EXPENSES	
Car payment	$
Gas and tolls	$
Car registration, insurance (annual payment divided by 12), and roadside assistance coverage	$
Maintenance and repairs	$
Public transportation	$
Subtotal: Transportation Expenses	$
ENTERTAINMENT EXPENSES	
Eating out	$
Events (concerts, museums, and shows)	$
Books, magazines, DVD rentals, software, and games	$
Vacation	$
Gifts	$
Hobbies (such as photography or quilting)	$
Subtotal: Entertainment Expenses	$
CHILD-RELATED EXPENSES (other than nanny care, or as needed for older children)	
Preschool, private school, college tuition, or college savings	$
School expenses	$
Classes and activities	$
Day care	$
Allowance	$
Support payments	$
Subtotal: Child-Related Expenses	$
REGULAR SAVINGS	
Rainy day or special event savings	$
Other savings	$
Subtotal: Regular Savings	$

Household Spending Plan (cont'd)	
MONTHLY EXPENSES (cont'd)	
Expense type	**Cost per month**
MISCELLANEOUS EXPENSES	
Legal or accounting fees	$
Gifts to charity	$
Other	$
Subtotal: Miscellaneous Expenses	$
OTHER MONTHLY DEBTS	
Credit card minimum payment	$
Student loans	$
Unpaid bills on repayment plans	$
Other	$
Subtotal: Other Monthly Debts	$
Total of expenses and debts	$
Difference between income and expenses	$

What's Left Over

Finally, subtract your total monthly expenses from the total net income you calculated earlier. Is the result enough to pay the average wage for a nanny? (We're hoping it's at least a positive number!)

If not, this budget exercise may have turned up spending patterns that you want to change. Start by examining purely discretionary expenses—those you don't have to pay, or perhaps for things you aren't really using, like cable TV. Many people can reduce what they spend on consumer goods, like electronics or clothes. With some trimming and shifting, your goal of hiring a nanny may be more reachable than you thought.

Hiring Part-Time Nanny Care

If the cost of hiring a nanny still seems out of your reach (or you simply don't need full-time child care coverage), you might instead hire a nanny part time. Any remaining hours during which you need child care could be filled in with either:

- less expensive forms of child care
- more of your own time (perhaps by cutting back on your work hours), or
- organized child care trades, classes, or play dates with other families.

We'll discuss these strategies below.

Be prepared for a bit of sticker shock, however. Part-time nannies earn more per hour than full-time nannies (even when you pay them a salary, rather than literally paying by the hour). This compensates them for the difficulty in finding a source of income to fill their remaining hours. Most part-time nannies want to work at least four hours at a stretch for a minimum of 12 to 15 hours each week. So you'll need to make sure that whatever form of child care fills the gap is inexpensive, to compensate for the premium wage you'll pay for part-time nanny care.

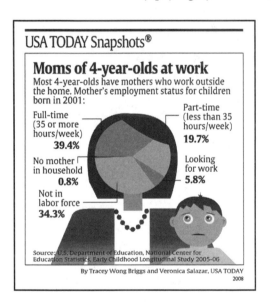

USA TODAY Snapshots®

Moms of 4-year-olds at work

Most 4-year-olds have mothers who work outside the home. Mother's employment status for children born in 2001:

Full-time (35 or more hours/week) **39.4%**

Part-time (less than 35 hours/week) **19.7%**

No mother in household **0.8%**

Looking for work **5.8%**

Not in labor force **34.3%**

Source: U.S. Department of Education, National Center for Education Statistics, Early Childhood Longitudinal Study 2005-06

By Tracey Wong Briggs and Veronica Salazar, USA TODAY 2008

An alternative to a part-time nanny is sharing one full-time nanny with another family, as described in Chapter 2. You could also simply help the nanny find another part-time job. Or, if you have space for a nanny to live in, there's nothing to stop you from offering this even if the nanny works only part time (reduce your salary accordingly).

Part-time nannies can be hard to find, however, because they're in high demand, especially since the recession began. Some parents report success by advertising at local colleges, where students need extra money and wouldn't be able to work full time anyway.

Supplementing Part-Time Nanny Help With Classes or Other Child Care

You may be able to find a day care or in-home care facility that accepts children for the morning or afternoon hours only, or for certain days per week. Or maybe one of your own parents or in-laws lives in the area and would be amenable to regularly scheduled time with a grandchild. If so, you can advertise for a nanny who will work the remaining hours.

Enrolling children in classes may also help take the load off. You've probably already seen classes advertised for kids of every age, whether it's to introduce them to music, physical fitness, or arts and crafts. If you don't see any advertised in your area, don't let that stop you. As Barry, a dad in Oakland, California, explains, "We found a local artist with a backyard studio who was both experienced in teaching children and willing to create a Friday afternoon art group for our and our friends' preschool and kindergarten age kids. The kids make art for a few hours, she feeds them milk and cookies, and we get a break!"

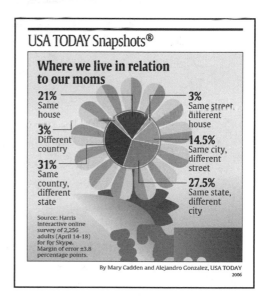

USA TODAY Snapshots®

Where we live in relation to our moms

21% Same house

3% Different country

31% Same country, different state

3% Same street, different house

14.5% Same city, different street

27.5% Same state, different city

Source: Harris Interactive online survey of 2,256 adults (April 14–18) for for Skype. Margin of error ±3.8 percentage points.

By Mary Cadden and Alejandro Gonzalez, USA TODAY 2006

You might even arrange to have the nanny pick your child up from day care or a class or drop the child off midday. This will free up even more of your day.

Should You Ask Grandparents to Fill In?

When Lynne Bolinger's daughter and son-in-law asked her to care for their two preschoolers for nine days last summer, she didn't hesitate to say yes: At 58, she's a healthy high school English teacher who walks an hour each day in her neighborhood in Kokomo, Indiana. And, she adores her grandsons.

But taking full care of 2-year-old Noah and 4-year-old Drew was hard work, Bolinger says: "I was doing all the Grandma things, like playing with the boys, but I was also doing all the Mommy things, like doing all the laundry and getting the meals. I could not believe how exhausted I was at the end of each day."

Millions of grandparents know just how she feels. They are regular or frequent babysitters for their grandchildren or, in a growing number of cases, share a home with grandchildren they care for—whether as a full-time substitute for a missing parent or as a senior member of a multigenerational household. Grandparent care often is good for children, studies show. But is it good for grandparents?

It can be, says Linda Waite, a professor of sociology at the University of Chicago and coauthor of a study of 12,872 grandparents. The study, published in 2007 in the *Journal of Gerontology: Social Science*, followed caregiving grandparents ages 50 to 80 for four years. Though previous, smaller studies had suggested they would see greater declines in health than their peers, this study found:

- no evidence that caring for grandkids 50 hours a year or more causes dramatic declines, and
- possible benefits for grandmothers who babysit 200 to 500 hours a year. They exercise more and get depressed less.

But it's not for everyone. Some grandparents are in poor health, have other things to do, or "just can't handle the noise and confusion," says Sharon Brangman, chief of geriatrics at SUNY Upstate Medical University in Syracuse, and a board member of the American Geriatrics Society. Others provide care despite risks to themselves

---

Should You Ask Grandparents to Fill In?, (cont'd)

or their grandchildren, she adds. "I've had grandparents who have memory problems and I've had to talk to parents and say, 'I don't feel this is safe.'"

Brangman's advice for parents and grandparents who are considering child care:

- Have a frank talk. Repeat every few months. Include touchy subjects, such as pay and driving.
- Make sure children and grandparents are up to date on vaccines, including flu vaccines.
- Have an alternate plan for when grandparents or kids get sick: Your child's cold could turn into a more serious illness in an elderly grandparent.

 Grandma on duty; Babysitting or fill-in parenting can be a blessing and a curse," by Kim Painter, January 5, 2009.

Spending More of Your Time at Home

You, along with your spouse or partner, have no doubt already considered either reducing your hours at work or trying to work at home. If you'd previously thought such options wouldn't work, now is a good time to reconsider. Even bosses who might not have been open to such an arrangement in the past may start noticing that flexible, family-friendly work schedules are the wave of the future. Or, the boss may be relieved, for financial reasons, to learn you're interested in cutting your hours.

Here are the most common alternative work arrangements and tips on making the most of them:

- **Working part time.** This means cutting your hours at work, for example to 60% time, which is typically enough for the employer to continue your health and other benefits. Take a careful look at your responsibilities and propose a plan to your boss in which you continue handling selected core tasks, but unload enough work that you don't get stuck doing a full-time job for part-time pay.

- **Working flex time.** This means shifting the hours when you work, for example from 12:30 to 8:30 instead of the usual 9:00 to 5:00. This can allow you to maintain your salary and hire a part-time nanny, or take a tag team approach to child care with your spouse or partner. Unlike many other options, flex time makes it visibly obvious to your boss and others that you're still working hard.

- **Working a compressed workweek.** Similar to flex time, this means doing the same job during different hours, but piling up a lot of hours on certain days. The classic example is arranging to work four ten-hour days instead of five eight-hour days, giving you one day a week off. Another good possibility is to work three ten-hour days and two five-hour days, giving you two afternoons off each week. Of course, these long days can be brutal, and mean many hours at a time away from your kids.

- **Teleworking.** Teleworkers do the same job in the same number of total hours, but from home or another remote location. It works best for office jobs, where you can connect with the office via computer and other electronic technology. Depending on how much regular phone or email contact your job requires during the business day, teleworking can give you a great deal of flexibility as to what hours you actually work. The biggest challenges are convincing your boss that you'll continue to get your work done— and then continuing to remind everyone of your high performance and eligibility for raises and promotions. Loneliness or longing for adult conversation can also be an issue, leading some parents to arrange part-time telework.

USA TODAY Snapshots®

Working remotely, vs. in the office

Do you think your work quality is perceived the same when you work remotely as when you are physically in the office?

Yes **55%**

No **45%**

Source: HotJobs survey of 1,465 workers. Margin of error: ±3 percentage points.

By Jae Yang and Karl Gelles, USA TODAY 2008

Work or Stay at Home? Moms Struggle Over Choices

Recent research reflects the ambivalence with which many mothers regard their own decisions about working or staying home, and many feel harshly judged for their choices.

"I often hear moms who are thinking of going back to work tell me they need flexibility, but being at home is driving them crazy," says Robin Ryan, a career coach and author of *What to Do with The Rest of Your Life*, in an email. "Stay-at-home moms complain a lot that 'just being a mom' is like being invisible in this society."

But working moms feel qualms about their choices, too. Christina Zola, 39, of Washington, DC, longs to stay home with her four-year-old son, Nicholas, but works full time doing marketing for an architecture firm.

"The guilt is there, wherever I am, and I rarely feel I'm in the right place at the right time," Zola says. "We all, as mothers, live with the consequences of our choices, and we don't take them lightly."

More prefer part-time jobs

In the span of the past decade, full-time work outside the home has lost some of its appeal to mothers, a report from the Pew Research Center found. This trend holds for mothers who have such jobs and those who don't.

Among working mothers with children 17 and under, one in five (21%) say full-time work is the ideal situation for them, down from the 32% who said that in 1997, according to a July 2007 Pew Research Center survey. Six in ten (up from 48% in 1997) of working mothers say part-time work would be their ideal, and one in five (19%) say they would prefer not working at all outside the home.

Mommy Wars—that often unspoken judgment that persists over the choices that both working and stay-at-home moms make—can be avoided if mothers become more comfortable about the choices they make and why they've made them, says Lynn Jarrett, a coach and author "Understand that every woman is 'wired' differently. Different

Work or Stay at Home? Moms Struggle Over Choices, (cont'd)

personalities have unique approaches and ideas on parenting," Jarrett says in an email. "There's no 'right' or 'wrong' answer, but what fits best for you and your family needs. Stop 'should-ing' on yourself."

 "Work or stay at home? It's still a quandary; Moms struggle with guilt over their choices," by Stephanie Armour, October 3, 2007.

TIP

About to have a new baby? Federal law guarantees eligible working parents 12 weeks of leave time after your child's birth, adoption, or foster placement. You've got up to a year in which to take advantage of this. Unfortunately, that leave is unpaid. The law is called the Family and Medical Leave Act (FMLA) and makes you eligible to claim this leave if you work for an employer with at least 50 employees, have worked there for a least one year, and worked at least 1,250 hours during that year. Also check your state's family leave law—it may be even more generous.

Supplementing Nanny Care With Child Care Trades With Other Parents

You're not the only parent who's looking for affordable child care. In fact, you probably won't have to look far to find others like you: Members of your prenatal group, neighbors, and other parents at the nearby park are probably all considering their options. Some may be open to a regularly scheduled arrangement in which you take care of each other's kids (sometimes referred to as a "babysitting cooperative").

This concept is a step more formal than scheduling alternating play dates. You might agree on a time—such as every Friday, or on regular weekday afternoons—and then trade off either delivering your kids to your friends' houses or waiting for them to drop their kids off at yours. If your schedules can't be predicted so readily, you might work out a system in which you keep track of the hours (or half hours) that you do child care for other parents, then create a point system that lets you keep the hours in balance.

The system of scheduling and point keeping that you choose might depend on the number of families in your group. Many groups start with two or three families. But once they've got the basic administration under control, some work their way up to as many as 25 families—

USA TODAY Snapshots®

Time vs. money
Young women say they are willing to take a pay cut to spend more time with their children:

No 11% Yes 89%

No 15% Yes 85% More than $50,000

No 6% Yes 94% $35,001–$50,000

No 14% Yes 86% $25,001–$35,000

$15,001–$25,000

No 18% Yes 82%

Less than $15,000

Source: Silver Stork Research Survey of 444 women ages 18 to 27 conducted in February. Margin of error ± 4 percentage points.

By Darryl Haralson and Frank Pompa, USA TODAY 2004

in which case, a system of flexible hours and times based on availability, plus tracking the number of hours that any one set of parents has given and received child care, tends to work best.

To create such a group, draw up a list of all the parents you know nearby, then figure out which ones meet all of the following criteria:

- You trust them to be responsible and nurturing with your children.

- Their home environment is safe and healthy (before raising the co-op possibility, you might do some reconnaissance; for example, schedule a play date at their house to give you an excuse to see it).

- One of them works at home or part time.

- Your kids and theirs get along well (if they're old enough for this to matter).

For more information on forming a babysitting co-op, see *The Sharing Solution*, by Janelle Orsi and Emily Doskow (Nolo).

> **CAUTION**
>
> **Make sure state law won't treat your co-op caregivers as "child care facilities."** In many states, anyone who provides care for more than a minimum number of children must obtain state licensing and follow various other rules. That's probably more than you want to deal with, so look up the law and organize your child care group so as to slip out from under its reach. See the state-by-state links to laws at the website of the National Resource Center for Health and Safety in Childcare and Early Education, http://nrckids.org (click "State Licensing and Regulation Information"). You may be able to get the information you need straight from the "Definitions" section

USA TODAY Snapshots®

Would you trust your boss to babysit your kids for a night?

Yes
72%

No **21%**

Not applicable/not sure
6%

Source: Marlin's 13th annual "Attitudes in the American Workplace" survey of 752 workers 18 and older. Margin of error ±4 percentage points.

By Jae Yang and Veronica Salazar, USA TODAY 2007

of the law. For example, Nevada's reads like this: "NAC 432A.050 'Child care center' defined. (NRS 432A.077) 'Child care center' means any facility in which the licensee regularly provides day or night care for more than 12 children."

Bartering Helps Lower Family's Child Care Costs

Cliff and Kara Petty learned that sometimes you can spend less—and gain much more.

USA TODAY and "Good Morning America Weekend" selected the Pettys of Sunrise, Florida, for the fifth and final Frugal Family Challenge, a 30-day exercise in saving money. The Challenge has helped ten families reduce their spending on everything from energy bills to groceries by hooking them up with financial advisers.

The Pettys' challenge: cut their child care costs, which averaged about $1,000 a month for after-school care, day care, and babysitting for their sons Aiden, six, and Landon, two.

Cliff, a firefighter, often works 24-hour shifts. Kara, interim director for Miami Gardens Parks and Recreation, works full time and sometimes has late-night meetings.

It was not unusual for the couple to hire a sitter up to three times a week to come to their house and watch their children.

The Frugal Family Challenge matched the Pettys with Sheila Marcelo, CEO of Care.com, which helps people find caretakers for children and pets. She suggested that the Pettys barter with friends and relatives for babysitting services instead of paying a private sitter and return the favor by babysitting their children on another date.

Cliff and Kara took her advice—recruiting not only Kara's sister, Angie Gonzalez, who lives about four miles away, but also friends, Cliff's brother and sister, and his parents.

Now, Landon and Aiden are more likely to be found splashing around with four cousins in their aunt's pool than with a sitter. Kara says for her sons, going to her sister's house is "like a big field trip."

And she has the assurance of quality child care that she can trust.

"It worked out for all of us," Kara says.

Cliff says bartering for child care made a big difference for him. "I didn't want to be that guy who's putting their kids on people," Cliff

Bartering Helps Lower Family's Child Care Costs, (cont'd)

says. There's no guilt, he says. "They were open to it because some-times they need a break, too."

When bartering time is not an option, Marcelo suggested that the Pettys have a sitter watch more kids than just their own—and share cost with other parents.

Over the month, the Pettys shaved about 20%, or $200, off their child care expenses. "It feels good," Cliff says, adding that they'll save the money or take a vacation.

Financial adviser Dave Moran, chairman of the Financial Planning Association of Miami-Dade, suggests they put that money toward retirement savings.

Marcelo notes that the Pettys "far exceeded their goal" of cutting their costs 10%. Next, she says, the Pettys should create a more formal way of tracking their time swaps, and, as an "insurance policy," line up substitute caregivers who have been vetted." It's those unplanned crises that result in high spending on child care," she says.

Kara and Cliff say they will follow up on the advice. But for now, they're thrilled they created lasting savings in a short time period.

"I couldn't be more happy; I think we balanced it right on the head," Cliff says.

 "Bartering helps lower family's child care costs," by Michelle Walbaum, June 19, 2009.

Sharing a Nanny With Another Family

Let's say you've decided you're ready to go back to work, and so has your friendly neighbor down the street. Both of you would like to hire a nanny, whether full time or part time. Does it make sense for each of you to hire separate nannies? Maybe not.

Sharing nanny care is a common solution to child care cost concerns. It can be structured in any number of ways, such as:

- full-time nanny care for both families' children at the same time (at one of your homes, or perhaps alternating between the two)

- part-time nanny care for your children on certain days and for the other family's children on other days, adding up to a full-time job, or

- part-time nanny care for your children on certain days, the other family's children on other days, but with each of you allowed to choose a certain number of hours or days during which the nanny cares for all the children simultaneously.

As you can see, a common goal when you're not both using the nanny full time is to create a full-time job for the nanny. That can allow you to keep costs down, because part-time nannies tend to charge more, due to the uncertainty of filling their leftover hours.

In this chapter, we'll take a closer look at the advantages and disadvantages of sharing nannies and then explain how to make this type of arrangement work.

Sharing a Nanny—Advantages and Disadvantages

Whether to share a nanny can be a tough decision; both the advantages and disadvantages are fairly extreme. Here's the basic breakdown, starting with these advantages:

- **Reduced salary.** In the most cost-effective situation, all your nanny hours will be shared with another parent, and you'll divide the nanny's salary in two. Although the nanny will want (and deserve) an overall higher salary for taking care of more children in total—especially if they're infants—you're still likely to realize a significant overall savings. (But you'll still be expected to pay more than if you were one family with the same number of kids, to compensate the nanny for the complexities that come with a share arrangement.)

At the other end of the spectrum, if the nanny is basically doing two part-time jobs and your children are never cared for at the same time, you still won't have to pay as much as if both sets of parents had hired part-time nannies.

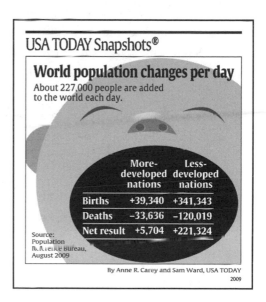

USA TODAY Snapshots®

World population changes per day

About 227,000 people are added to the world each day.

	More-developed nations	Less-developed nations
Births	+39,340	+341,343
Deaths	−33,636	−120,019
Net result	+5,704	+221,324

Source: Population Reference Bureau, August 2009

By Anne R. Carey and Sam Ward, USA TODAY 2009

- **Split costs of benefits.** Expenses beyond salary will be lower in a shared situation. Susan, in Washington, DC, points out, "Covering a nanny's health insurance can be quite expensive, but by sharing the nanny with another family, we were able to provide this benefit." The same goes for year-end bonuses, and any other perks you might provide, such as coverage of commute costs or even everyday snacks.

- **Nearly all of the advantages of hiring a nanny.** Your child will get lots of personal attention, in a comfortable setting at a home— quite possibly your own home, depending on the agreement between you and the other family. The children probably won't get sick as often as kids in day care. And if you're delivering your child to the other house, no one will be upset if you're a little late (though you shouldn't abuse this flexibility, especially not at the end of the day when the other family is ready to have the house to themselves).

- **Playmates for your children.** If you arrange for simultaneous nanny care and your children and the share family's children get along well, they'll have standing play dates. If they're old enough to play together with minimal supervision, that can take the load off your nanny to provide constant entertainment (reducing the chances that she'll get tired and resort to turning on the television). But don't expect the nanny to redirect her energies toward housework; that's a lot to ask when more than one child is involved.

- **Someone to share the role of employer.** For many parents, a nanny is the first person they've ever needed to hire and supervise. Even when you're trying to do it right, it can be helpful to have someone to compare notes with. In an ideal situation, your share family will become close friends, as well. And if the nanny gets sick, odds are that one out of the various parents in the share will be able to step in and provide childcare that day.

Now, for the disadvantages:

- **Lots to agree on.** A number of decisions lie ahead of you, such as what hours the nanny will work, how much you'll pay, when and whether the nanny will merit a raise, what form of discipline should be used for the kids, how often she should take them for field trips, how strictly nap time or limitations on watching TV should be enforced, and more. With a nanny share, you'll have to agree on most or all of these things with the other family (depending, of course, on how much the care of your children overlaps).

- **Inevitable scheduling complications.** Even after both families have agreed on the hours the nanny will work, there will probably be times when someone needs an adjustment, such as a late start on a certain day. If that messes up the other family's schedule, tensions can rise. Amy, in Seattle, says "We dealt with some scheduling issues by simply paying our nanny for a little more time than she was regularly expected to be there, with the understanding that this would cover the days when one of us was late returning from work."

- **Vacation issues.** Traditionally, you have to pay the nanny even when you're on vacation (for reasons we'll discuss in Chapter 4). The nanny herself also gets a certain number of days of paid vacation. Of course, many families try to plan their vacation to coincide with the nanny's—but that gets harder with another family in the mix.

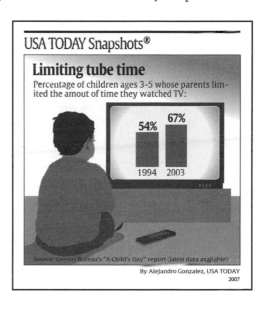

USA TODAY Snapshots®

Limiting tube time

Percentage of children ages 3-5 whose parents limited the amout of time they watched TV:

54% — 1994
67% — 2003

Source: Census Bureau's "A Child's Day" report (latest data available)

By Alejandro Gonzalez, USA TODAY
2007

- **Breaking up will be hard to do.** Even if everything works out with the shared nanny for several months, one family may want to put their child into another form of care sooner than the other—leaving the other family scrambling to find a share family that's a similarly good match. And in a worst-case scenario, one of you will be dissatisfied with a nanny that the other one likes (perhaps because the nanny clicks with only one of your children).

Setting up a Share Arrangement

To make this work, you'll need to:

- Find a family to share with.
- Find the right nanny.
- Put your agreement with the other family into written form.

We'll cover all of this in this section or, where appropriate, in subsequent chapters.

Finding Your Perfect-Match Share Family

We've deliberately put this as the first step, because it's easier to find a family interested in joining with you on a search for a shared nanny than it is to first find a nanny and then find a family who is not only happy to share with you, but also happy with the nanny you've chosen. (And what if the nanny doesn't like the second family or their children?)

To find potential share families, your best bets include:

- **Asking around.** Neighbors, friends, pleasant-looking families in the local tot park—any of these might either offer leads on someone interested in a nanny share or be interested themselves. If you're a member of Facebook or other social networking sites, mention your search there.

- **Posting an ad.** Include some basic details in your ad, like what area you live in and how many days a week you'd like to share. No need to go for big-newspaper classifieds on this one. Post flyers in local stores and other places parents might visit, and use free online resources like Craigslist.

- **Check the ads yourself.** You may spot another family in your area who's already looking. They may, in fact, already have a nanny, especially if their former share family has moved on. If you don't like the nanny, of course it's a no-go. But if you do, you'll have found a nanny that one family, at least, has been pleased with, for minimal effort.

Don't just say yes to the first family whose schedule fits yours, however. It's important to spend time ensuring that your personalities and priorities are truly in sync. If you haven't yet met in person, start with a phone conversation covering the basics. If that goes well, arrange to meet in one of your homes.

Although part of the purpose of the in-home meeting should be unstructured getting-to-know-you time, you should also discuss both of your approaches and preferences regarding the following:

- care schedule
- whose house the nanny and kids will use, and when

- nap times
- food preferences
- activities (both recommended, like trips to the library, and prohibited, like videogames or playing with toy guns)
- other matters of personal philosophy
- nonnegotiable preferences regarding the nanny (such as gender, educational background or CPR certification, non-smoking, drivers' license, language ability, or even religion), and
- what you're willing to offer the nanny in terms of pay (under the table or not?), vacation and other benefits, reimbursements, and eventual raises and bonuses.

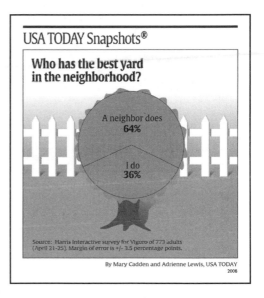

USA TODAY Snapshots®

Who has the best yard in the neighborhood?

A neighbor does
64%

I do
36%

Source: Harris Interactive survey for Vigoro of 773 adults (April 21-25). Margin of error is +/- 3.5 percentage points.

By Mary Cadden and Adrienne Lewis, USA TODAY 2008

If both families still seem compatible, arrange to have your children meet on another day. Of course, if you get home and have second thoughts, you can also bow out gracefully at this point.

TIP
Somewhere during this process, make sure you see the other family's home. Unless your child will never set foot there, you want to make sure it's clean, roomy, and childproofed, and perhaps has some outdoor play space or features anything else that's important to you and your child.

Finding the Nanny

To locate, screen, and hire an excellent nanny, you'll need to follow the steps described in Chapters 6, 7, and 9—but with a difference. Both families should take part in all but the most basic parts of the process, to avoid early misunderstandings. Even if all goes well during the hiring process, you don't want one family, down the line, to be able to say, "Well, you hired her, so you deal with that!"

Start this process as soon as you can, even if you won't need the care to begin for a while. Some families report that it took them months to find a nanny they both agreed on.

If at all possible, choose a nanny who has been part of a sharing arrangement or something similar before. That way, she'll be comfortable with the juggling aspects of it and may even suggest ways to make it work better. If the selection of potential nannies isn't that wide, look for one who has cared for more than one child at a time. Caring for two children is often more than twice the work of caring for one.

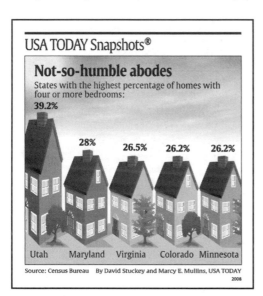

USA TODAY Snapshots®

Not-so-humble abodes

States with the highest percentage of homes with four or more bedrooms:

39.2% Utah
28% Maryland
26.5% Virginia
26.2% Colorado
26.2% Minnesota

Source: Census Bureau   By David Stuckey and Marcy E. Mullins, USA TODAY
2008

According to Amy, the mother of two boys in Seattle, "After my first son was born and my brother's family and mine started looking for a shared nanny, we had trouble finding one who was willing. My brother at that time had two kids in elementary school and a one-year old. The nanny needed to get his older two kids off to school, then spend the balance of the day with the two one-year olds. Fortunately, we found a nanny who had run a daycare center and was completely unfazed by the number of kids. She stayed with us for five years, continuing on after I had my second son."

CAUTION

You may need to get licensed as a group day-care facility.
Some states' laws require this for shared-care arrangements. You can
try researching this yourself via the website of the National Resource
Center for Health and Safety in Childcare and Early Education, http://
nrckids.org (click "State Licensing and Regulation Information").
However, this information may be hard to find. An easier route may
be calling the appropriate regulatory agency in your state; find out the
number by calling the same Resource Center at 800-598-KIDS.

Putting Your Agreement With Your Share Family in Writing

Don't be nervous, we're not suggesting that you call in the lawyers and
create a multipage tome. But memories are short (and self-serving),
and a day may come when one
or both of you need a solid
reminder of what you said
originally. Besides, you may
have already misunderstood the
other and not known it—it's
amazing what comes out when
you put something down
on paper. Below is a sample
agreement for use by the parents
covering the major logistical
and philosophical issues.

Notice that we've suggested
waiting until your actual nanny
has been chosen. You can
also write up an agreement before that—but if the nanny negotiates
different terms, you'll have to come back and change it. Note also that
this is separate from any written material or agreements you give to the
nanny (discussed in Chapter 9).

USA TODAY Snapshots®

Safety precautions at home

Percentage of adults in the USA who have:

Smoke alarms
96%

Fire extinguishers
80%

Carbon monoxide
detectors
46%

Source: 2006 Fire Safety Census, a telephone survey of 1,005 adults
25 and older conducted in August 2006 by KRC Research for Liberty
Mutual and International Association of Fire Fighters. Margin of error
±3.1 percentage points.

By Tracey Wong Briggs and Veronica Salazar, USA TODAY
2008

Nanny-Share Agreement Between Parents

Clark and Nancy Fellow, living at 811 Ocean Place, Sequim, Washington, and Charlie and Serena Eggbetter, living at 244 Seaside Drive, Sequim, Washington, agree as follows:

That we will jointly hire a nanny, Maria Cancino, for our children, Mira Fellow and Inga Eggbetter. The nanny will work daily from 8:30 a.m. to 5:30 p.m., in the Fellows' home except as provided below.

The Eggbetter's child will go to the Fellow's house to receive care from Monday through Thursday (except when the Fellows are on vacation or their daughter is ill and contagious, in which case the nanny will come to the Eggbetters' house). Both families will follow the schedule as closely as possible and make all reasonable efforts to advise the other family in advance when a schedule change is required.

The nanny's responsibilities for the children include the following (with exceptions for bad weather or other extenuating circumstances): playing with and reading to them, ensuring that they nap every day according to schedules provided by the parents, taking them to story time at the library every Tuesday afternoon, preparing and feeding them lunch and snacks, and changing their diapers. Watching television or videos (child-appropriate programs only) is to be limited to three hours per week.

At the end of each Thursday, when the Eggbetters arrive to pick up Inga, both families will set aside an additional half hour after the nanny has left to share information about the nanny and children's week and to discuss any issues regarding the sharing arrangement. The families will meet jointly with the nanny every three months for a performance review.

The nanny's salary will be $500 per week. Of this, the Fellows will pay $200 and the Eggbetters will pay $300. The families will each pay the nanny their share of the salary every two weeks, by separate checks. Each family will deduct and pay a share of payroll taxes. The families will also pay workers' compensation insurance, after researching the laws in our state.

Nanny-Share Agreement Between Parents (cont'd)

In addition, the Eggbetters will pay the Fellows $50 per week as compensation for the food, diapers, and other supplies that Inga eats or uses during the day. Before the nanny is actually hired, we will discuss and decide on what foods we agree are nutritious and acceptable for the children to eat.

If the Fellows' daughter, Mira, contracts a contagious illness, the nanny will instead come to the Eggbetters' house to care for their daughter, Inga, alone. If Inga contracts a contagious illness, she will stay home. However, both families will owe the nanny the same weekly salary regardless of illness.

The nanny will receive five days of paid sick leave and two weeks of paid vacation per year and be required to give both families a minimum of two months' notice before taking a vacation. In addition, the nanny will receive all federal holidays except for Columbus Day and New Year's Eve.

Each family will, to the extent possible, give the other at least one month's notice of their vacation or travel schedules, for coordination purposes. In any case, each family will owe the nanny the same amount regardless of vacation or other days of unused care.

The two families will discuss at the end of one year whether the nanny's performance merits a bonus, gift, and/or a raise.

If disputes arise between the families that we are unable to resolve, we will go to mediation at our local Community Mediation Services, with costs to be shared equally between the families, before ending this agreement.

If one family wishes to end this shared-care arrangement, it will give the other family a minimum of four weeks' notice and provide two weeks' pay for the nanny. If a family gives less notice it will be responsible for paying its full normal share of the nanny's salary until the proper notice date.

⊘ **CAUTION**
You won't always see eye to eye with your share family. Dalia, of Fremont, California, explains, "Our nanny share mostly worked out fine, but there was one thing about the other family I could never understand: They refused to give the nanny a key to their house. That led to some awkward situations where she got locked out. Why would you trust someone with your child whom you wouldn't trust with your house?"

Both at the beginning and throughout your sharing relationship, communication with your share family and the nanny is key. Talking out details of your expectations or impressions early on can help prevent major disputes later. You'll notice that in the sample agreement, the family scheduled regular meetings with each other. This isn't always necessary, but some formal process for information sharing is a good idea—even if it's only a dedicated notebook or pad of paper left in an obvious place in which each you each write notes to the others.

Dissolving a Sharing Agreement

One of these days, months, or years, one of your or the share family's kids won't need the nanny anymore. Perhaps one of you will move to a different neighborhood, get a new job that offers in-house daycare, or simply decide to try another form of child care.

If you're the "breakup victim," try to look at it philosophically—one of you was bound to want out before the other. Then turn your energies to finding another family to share with. Just as with your initial search, you'll want to ask around and post ads, both in the form of flyers and online. Be sure to ask the departing family whether they know of any likely share families (unless the parting wasn't amicable).

Finding a new family to share with can be harder than finding the initial share family, because you're probably hoping to stay as close to your original arrangement as possible, while the other family may prefer another setup. And the other family has to like not only you and your kids (who are older by now, and perhaps more rambunctious), but your nanny.

Many parents have had to bite the bullet and pay the nanny's full salary while they were looking for a family to share with. That's what happened to Amyb, when her brother and family went to Norway for a year. She says, "The stability was worth it, but it was a tough year financially." ●

Who's Your Ideal Nanny?
Listing Priorities

Y ou probably have a picture in your mind of the perfect nanny—someone nurturing and creative, able to laugh with you and your children, and able to graciously take a load of work off your shoulders.

But what does that mean in literal terms? Unless you expect to post an ad that says simply, "Wanted: Nice Nanny," that's exactly what this chapter will help you figure out.

The Credentials and Experience Your Nanny Should Have

Let's start with the basics: What should your nanny bring to the table (or playroom)? You might aim for any or all of the following:

- **Experience caring for children.** The ideal for most parents is someone who has worked as a nanny and cared for the same age and number of children as yours. Understandably, the most experienced nannies get snapped up fast (and for the highest pay). Some likely compromises include a nanny who has raised children of her own or at least been the favorite aunt to a lot of children; a former teacher; or even an immigrant with nursing or medical training who isn't yet licensed to practice in the United States.

- **Education and training.** Career nannies sometimes have a degree, such as a B.A. in early childhood education. Expect to pay a premium for that, however. First aid training and infant and child CPR are basic qualifications that should not, however, add significantly to the cost. (Or you can pay for the training yourself; the course is fairly short.) What about a high school diploma? You'll probably be approached by applicants who don't have one. While their lack of knowledge of U.S. history or geometry probably won't affect their basic ability as caregivers, you're within your rights to examine their ability to commit to a project and follow written and verbal instructions. Also, if you expect the nanny to provide help with homework, you're far better off if she has completed high school.

- **Drivers' license and car.** Unless your children are infants, you probably don't want them trapped at home all day. Is your neighborhood walkable (including to kid-friendly destinations like a park or library)? If not, the nanny will either need to take your kids on the bus or drive, using her car or yours. And that raises some obvious safety issues. For one, if she'll be using her car, you'll want to make sure it's safe, reasonably clean, and either already outfitted with car seats or can be outfitted with seats that you provide. She'll also need to have proper auto insurance (as discussed in Chapter 5).

- **Language proficiency.** For your sake as well as your children's, do your best to find a nanny who speaks English well. Many parents end up compromising on this requirement, given the large number of immigrants seeking work as nannies. In fact, some parents are excited by the prospect of their child learning another language early on, when the mind, ear, and tongue are most receptive. But this doesn't always work out. For example, Sandra, in Oregon, discovered that, "my nanny's English was so rudimentary that she simply didn't talk to the baby, who was spending entire days in silence." Inadequate stimulation like this is one of the most common causes of language delay. Children start listening well before they're able to speak, absorbing the foundation for their own language skills. Whether or not you'd like your children to become bilingual, try to aim for at least conversational English ability in your nanny and reasonable reading and writing skills. This is particularly important in case of an emergency—for example, if your allergic child were to eat a peanut at the park, you'd want a nanny who could quickly explain to people what's happening and call emergency personnel with a clear description of where she is and what she needs.

CAUTION
Remember, you'll have to talk to the nanny, too. As Shelly in Virginia, explains, "At first, I thought, 'What does English language ability really matter?' But I've learned over the years that it's really hard to convey certain nuances through language barriers. Our first au pair was new to child care, and I spent many hours every night talking through the day: What had happened, how did she handle it, what did she say, and so forth. It was hard to know whether we were really understanding each other."

- **U.S. work authorization.** Again, given the likelihood that you'll be interviewing immigrants, you'll need to decide whether they must be allowed to work here. If you decide to forego the immigration rules, the nanny will most likely want to be paid under the table—for reasons that you'll better understand after reading Chapter 5. Even if you decide to go that route, realize that a nanny who isn't in the United States legally may be deported at any time and will be unable to accompany you to places where identification documents might be checked, like across the U.S. border or on a plane or train.

- **Ability to cook.** If your nanny will be preparing food for your child or for you, you might want to ensure that she's capable of more than heating up ramen noodles or putting frozen food in the microwave.

- **Physical fitness.** You don't need to hire a marathon runner, but a nanny who is seriously out of shape won't be able to run around with—or after—your kids. This may be an even greater concern if you have a child with special needs.

- **Specialized knowledge or abilities.** If your child is disabled or requires injections, you may need someone with special skills. Or if, for example, you'd like your nanny to drive the children around in the family truck, you'll need to make sure she knows how. The same is true if you have horses, a house on the waterfront or with a pool, and so forth.

How About a Manny?

More men are finding careers as librarians, secretaries, nannies, pre-school teachers, nurses, paralegals, typists, dressmakers—even lactation consultants or midwives.

The transition is driven in part by mounting unemployment. The flimsy economic recovery makes more employees willing to consider new careers, even in fields that have long been considered women's work.

The change has brought about new slang, such as "mannies" for male nannies and "murses" for male nurses. It's brought about new, and sometimes unwanted, portrayals in the media: Ben Stiller's character, a male nurse, is the target of derision for his career choice in the movie *Meet the Parents*.

Fifty-eight percent of families would not consider hiring a man to provide in-home care for their children, according to a 2002 survey by Clifton Park, New York-based household tax and payroll services provider GTM Associates. While a female nanny might take five or ten interviews to land a job, her male counterpart can require dozens of meetings with prospective families before being hired.

While many find acceptance, some men in jobs long held by women still grapple with barriers that are too taboo to be spoken about on the job.

Experts in gender studies say men who work in child care might be viewed as potential molesters or criminals; those who work in health care, especially in areas such as maternity or gynecology, might be seen as voyeurs. Some men in female-oriented jobs say they get questioned about their sexual orientation.

 "More men train to be nurses, midwives, secretaries," by Stephanie Armour, July 11, 2003.

- **A particular gender.** The vast majority of nannies are women, and many parents still have trouble getting used to the idea of a male nanny. There is nothing legally wrong with deciding you'd prefer one gender over another.

- **Amenability to pets.** If you have cats, dogs, rabbits, or anything furry—or plan to get a pet—you'll need, at a minimum, to make sure the nanny won't be allergic. A few nannies might be willing to take the dog out while they're with the kids, but don't expect this. Some people are simply afraid of dogs, which could be a problem that affects your kids' interaction with the dog—or the nanny.

Live-In or Live-Out?

Most nannies have a home and perhaps a family of their own, to which they want to return at the end of the day. But for some families and nannies, a live-in setup works best all around, either during weekdays or all week long. The advantages to you include:

- **Help at odd hours.** If, for example, your work schedule is unpredictable or includes out-of-town travel, or your child needs late-night bottle feedings or diaper changes, you can arrange to have a live-in nanny handle care at these times. But notice that we didn't say "help at all hours." Your nanny's hours must still be limited (usually to between 8 and 12 per day, for a total of 40 and 60 a week), and you must make it clear when she's "on the clock."

- **Lower pay.** Room and board are valuable to some nannies, and they're willing to lower their rate of pay in return—customarily around 5% to 10% less. This can be handy if you've tied up all your money buying a good-sized house.

- **No problems with tardiness or no shows.** You'll never have to wonder whether your nanny is late for a good reason or simply decided she didn't feel like working anymore. Barring the unlikely possibility that she'll slip out the window late one night, you'll know just where to find her. (Then again, you may have to wake her up if she has overslept.)

- **Closer bond with your child.** A live-in nanny starts to feel almost like a member of the family (for better and for worse). To the child, that can be a positive thing, offering continuity and a sense that the nanny isn't just someone who inserts herself into the child's life, asks for respect and affection, then disappears at the end of the day.

Of course, there are disadvantages to you as well, including:

- **Loss of privacy.** You'll basically have a tenant in your home, who will see you in your pajamas, overhear your arguments, worry about the smell of smoke if you light a candle in your bedroom, and make you feel like you're never really alone.

- **Loss of space.** That extra bedroom might have been handy for your home office or for putting up out-of-town guests.

- **Getting to know the nanny's personal issues.** A nanny who can leave your house at the end of the day probably has

USA TODAY Snapshots®

The pet story

Total number of pets owned in the USA (in millions):

Fish — 148.6
Cats — 90.5
Dogs — 73.9
Small animals — 18.2
Birds — 16.6
Reptiles — 11

Source: American Pet Product Manufacturers Association

By David Stuckey and Marcy E. Mullins, USA TODAY
2007

other people to turn to when she's got boyfriend trouble, health concerns, or other issues. But if the nanny lives with you, you may be the first person she turns to—especially if she's young and just finding her way in the world. Finding a nanny who's a complete recluse isn't the answer. Katherine Robinson, founder of Beacon Hill Nannies in Boston, which places high-end nannies, told USA TODAY that one executive couple insisted on a nanny with "no personal or social life." Robinson asked them: "So you want Jeffrey Dahmer?"

Whether a nanny is willing to live in your house is an issue she probably won't have to think about too hard—she'll probably either like the idea or say "no way." Many nannies can't be parted from their own families for that long. But some nannies will jump at the idea because it:

- **Provides needed housing.** Many nannies are young, new to the United States, or without ready financial resources. A decent place to live is usually one of the biggest items in anyone's budget. If you have a good-sized house in a pleasant neighborhood, the nanny may delight in this instant upgrade to her circumstances. Even if she has a place to stay on the weekend, it may be jam-packed with friends or family. (Of course, she still deserves some privacy in your house, such as her own room and bathroom with locks on the doors.) This benefit becomes less valuable, however, if you want the nanny only on weekdays but she has no place to stay on weekends.

- **Provides food.** Providing a room means providing board, as well. Although food is a smaller part of the nanny's personal budget, it can add up. And it's a tangible perk that most everyone loves to receive.

- **Avoids a long commute.** There's every possibility that you and your chosen nanny live far away from each other. Commuting can add hours to an already tiring day.

- **Provides other perks.** Because a live-in nanny becomes an integral part of the family unit, it's traditional to offer her other perks, such as use of the family car (even during off hours), a gym membership, payment of costs to accompany you on family vacations, or even reimbursement for her solo travels to visit family or take some time off. Any such perks should be negotiated up front, although you can always throw in something else later.

Beyond the Basics: What Else Do You Expect?

You may have expectations that go beyond a nanny's basic abilities or capacities described above. For example, you may want the nanny to:

- **Work an unusual schedule.** Do you need the nanny to work full time or part time, on a set schedule, or within a range of times? Is it important for you to know that she'll be able to work on certain holidays (perhaps Thanksgiving morning, while you prepare to host), or occasionally on weekends or out-of-town trips with your family? Even if you plan on having a live-in nanny, you'll need to establish a regular schedule of either full-time or part-time hours: She can't be expected to work round the clock and will be owed overtime once you reach certain limits per day or week (as discussed in Chapter 5).

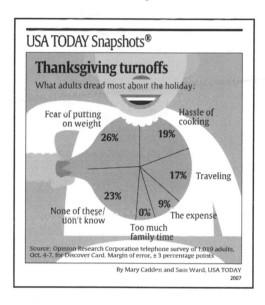

USA TODAY Snapshots®

Thanksgiving turnoffs

What adults dread most about the holiday:

Fear of putting on weight 26%

Hassle of cooking 19%

Traveling 17%

None of these/ don't know 23%

Too much family time 0%

The expense 9%

Source: Opinion Research Corporation telephone survey of 1,019 adults, Oct. 4-7, for Discover Card. Margin of error, ± 3 percentage points

By Mary Cadden and Sam Ward, USA TODAY 2007

TIP

Don't expect the nanny to depart the second you get home. You'll need to build at least 15 minutes into her regular schedule for you to talk about how things went that day.

- **Make a long-term commitment to the job.** This is high on the priority list for most parents, who don't want to worry that they'll train a nanny and get the kids accustomed to her only to have her take off in a few months. It's a valid concern: As Jack, a parent in Berkeley, California, found when interviewing nannies, "I was bothered by how many of them clearly saw being a nanny as slumming it—just a way to make some cash until a better prospect came along. To me, having my kids well cared for is the most important job in the world, and we were prepared to negotiate good terms—but only if the nanny would stay around for at least a year, to make it worth our while." Of course, no nanny can guarantee she'll stay for as long as you want, but in discussing her past work history and life goals, you'll be able to get a sense of whether she is serious about making a long-term career of child care. Be careful not to promise the nanny that she will have a job for a set length of time—we'll talk in Chapter 9 about preserving and communicating your right to let the nanny go at any time and for any reason.

- **Take your child to and from extracurricular activities.** Whether or not you require the nanny to have a car, she'll need to know how many days a week your child goes to classes or activities and what her pickup and delivery obligations will be.

- **Do household chores.** Most parents expect the nanny to perform a reasonable number of tasks directly connected to the child, such as preparing and cleaning up after meals or crafts and games, doing the child's laundry, generally tidying up after the child (or teaching the child to pitch in on this), and even shopping for milk or other food or snacks that the child needs. Some nannies are willing to do more, however, especially if you've got only one child, who can be relied on to take naps. For example, some will cook dinner for the family or do everyone's laundry. This depends completely on the nanny, however, and you may need to pay extra for such services.

TIP

Some nannies insist on cleaning! Karla, in Ardmore, Pennsylvania, says, "Our first nanny would not sit down. I told her it was okay to do whatever she wanted when the baby was napping, but instead she'd clean the kitchen, put the toys away, even scrub the bathroom if she had time." Tina, in Virginia, echoes: "Our nanny offered to do some light housework, but every now and then she'd do something dramatic, like attack a closet and take everything out and reorganize it, or take the slipcovers off my sofa and stick them in the washing machine. I loved this, especially because it all worked out (thankfully, the slipcovers turned out to be machine washable)."

- **Take care of errands.** If your nanny is already out and about with your child, there may be no harm in asking her to pick up the dry cleaning or drop off a library book along the way. But many nannies are familiar with the syndrome in which busy parents start asking more and more of the nanny, and the errands start to take over her day. Try to plan in advance what you'll expect of the nanny, then let her know. If you work long hours and really need her to regularly do errands, this can be negotiated. (But how much time do you really want your kid spending in a car seat, tagging along on errands?)

USA TODAY Snapshots®

Preparing meals

How much time people spend on daily meal preparation.

- 1/2 to 1 hour **28%**
- 1/2 hour or less **23%**
- Not sure **1%**
- None **6%**
- Over 3 hours **7%**
- 1 to 3 hours **35%**

Source: Harris Interactive telephone survey of 1,011 adults for Hormel Foods Corporation

By Michelle Healy and Sam Ward, USA TODAY 2008

- **Take care of friends' children at times.** If you regularly host play dates during nanny hours, without those kids' parents being present, you can't expect the nanny to automatically build responsibility for these extra kids into her duties. If it's a regular event, such as once a week, you might just build this into her salary. If not, it's simplest to separately pay the nanny a little extra for those hours.

> **TIP**
> **You may get tired of the nanny's cooking.** Dan, a father in Queens, New York, says, "At first, when our Chinese nanny began, I couldn't believe my luck: A tasty, multicourse Chinese meal every night! But after a year or so, I now dream of sneaking out for tacos. And we've been trying to teach her to cook some basic Western food, like spaghetti."

- **Share the house with a work-at-home parent.** As Jennifer, from San Mateo County, California, remembers, "One woman I was interviewing specifically asked the question, 'Will you be in the home when I'm here?' and before I had a chance to tell her that I work at home, she said 'I'm not comfortable with that.' That made me wonder what she had to hide." Although some nannies might feel like they're being monitored, others note that it can be hard to deal with separation anxiety among children old enough to know that Mommy or Daddy is just on the other side of that door or to discipline them if they believe they'll get let off the hook by a nearby parent.

- **Accompany your family on vacations.** If you already know that you'll want your nanny to go with you on family camping trips or other vacations, you'll need to be clear about that up front. And although the nanny should be comfortable with and interested in the prospect, don't expect her to regard it as a perk. Experienced nannies know that it's hard to appreciate a week in London if they're in the store trying to remember the British word for diapers (that's "nappies") while the parents hit the museums, or they're stuck playing patty-cake in the hotel room while the parents enjoy a Shakespeare play. We'll discuss taking vacations with a nanny more in Chapter 10.

- **Spend a lot of time outdoors with your child.** If you're serious about getting your child to enjoy outdoor activities, you'll want a nanny who is happy to push a stroller on walks, go to the park, and otherwise encourage the child to stop looking longingly at the TV. The nanny's enthusiasm for such activities is doubly important if you don't have a yard to play in.

- **Provide homework assistance.** If your children are school age and need school help beyond a little prodding, you'll need to find a nanny who speaks English and is comfortable in a tutoring role.

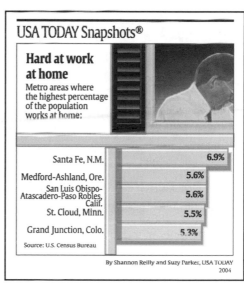

USA TODAY Snapshots®

Hard at work at home

Metro areas where the highest percentage of the population works at home:

Santa Fe, N.M.	6.9%
Medford-Ashland, Ore.	5.6%
San Luis Obispo-Atascadero-Paso Robles, Calif.	5.6%
St. Cloud, Minn.	5.5%
Grand Junction, Colo.	5.3%

Source: U.S. Census Bureau

By Shannon Reilly and Suzy Parker, USA TODAY
2004

- **Put up with other household quirks.** If anything else about your house is unusual—a roaming pet snake, an elderly parent receiving separate care, or whatever—think about how an outsider will react, and be sure to warn her.

By considering all of these issues in advance, you'll be in a much better position to talk meaningfully with prospective nannies about what the job entails and whether they're ready for it. And the nanny that you do hire won't face the shock of discovering unexpected responsibilities or burdens.

Checklist of Nanny Qualifications and Responsibilities

We want our nanny to:

☐ have at least the following amount of childcare experience:

_____

_____

☐ have at least the following amount of education:_____

_____

☐ have infant and child CPR training

☐ have a driver's license

☐ have her own car for use with our children

☐ pick up or deliver our child to the following activities on the
   following days: _____

_____

☐ be fluent (or at least proficient) in English

☐ be fluent in the following other language: _____

☐ be authorized to work in the United States

☐ know how to cook

☐ be comfortable with our pets

☐ be physically fit enough to care for a small child

☐ have the following additional special skills:_____

_____

_____

☐ live in our house

☐ work the following schedule: _____

_____

☐ do the following household chores: _____

_____

_____

Checklist of Nanny Qualifications and Responsibilities, (cont'd)

☐ regularly take care of the following errands: _____

_____

_____

☐ regularly take care of other children

☐ be willing to provide care while one of us is also at home

☐ be willing to accommodate the following other household
characteristics: _____

_____

_____

After filling in this list (or creating one of your own), draw an arrow toward the items that are particularly important to you and that you wouldn't wish to compromise on for any reason. ●

What's Fair, Yet Affordable?
Pay, Vacation, Other Terms

Your nanny will be performing one of the most important jobs in the world: helping raise your little ones and, keeping them healthy, clean, and happy. And you'd no doubt love to pay her every cent that she deserves and then some. Having worked out your budget in Chapter 1, you've probably got a good idea of what you can comfortably pay. But be prepared for the possibility of sticker shock.

In this chapter, we'll take a closer look at how the amount you'd like to pay matches up with local market realities and how to devise an attractive package of not only pay, but vacation and benefits.

High Enough, But Not Too High: Setting the Pay Rate

The amount you're offering to pay is, understandably, one of the primary things a nanny will consider when thinking about your offer (though it's not the only thing). So let's take a closer look at setting that amount, including:

- whether to pay a set amount or base your pay on hours worked
- how to research local rates
- how to settle on a range that you'll offer, and
- planning ahead for raises and bonuses.

In the discussion of nanny salaries that follows, we'll be talking about gross pay, that is, pretax wage amounts, for the simple reason that pay rates are usually advertised this way, whether for nannies or any other workers. Unfortunately, federal and state taxes will take a bite out of this amount—up to 20% of the nanny's pay. So, unless you plan to operate under the table, you'll need to make very clear to your nanny—who may not be sophisticated about such matters—that the amount she'll see in her paycheck will be lowered by the tax you have to withhold on her behalf (discussed in Chapter 5).

Preset Wage Versus Hourly Wage

The first thing to consider is whether you'll pay your nanny a fixed amount (probably every week) or an amount that's literally based on the number of hours she works (also calculated and paid every week). For most parents, the fixed arrangement works best. That's because it's predictable, lets the nanny know how much she'll make each week (even if it's for part-time work), and results in paying less per hour than a straight hourly wage. (We're not calling the fixed amount a "salary," for employment law reasons—please read "Why You Can't Pay Your Nanny a True 'Salary,'" below.)

Why You Can't Pay Your Nanny a True "Salary"

Only a few categories of workers—in many cases, professional workers—are legally entitled to receive a true "salary," meaning they receive the same amount of money no matter how many hours they work. Many professionals complain that they end up working very long hours indeed, but that's tough luck—their pay is supposed to be high enough to reflect that, and the laws don't grant them any right to overtime. Another word for this is that they are "exempt" employees.

Nannies, however, are normally considered "nonexempt" employees, meaning that if they work extra hours, both federal and, in some cases, state laws give them a right to be paid overtime. (The exception is live-in nannies, who are not entitled to overtime.)

One important caution when paying your nanny: If the nanny's regular weekly paycheck will include money for some overtime hours (for example, if you stay at the office late every Tuesday), be sure to sign something with her that explains your agreement regarding the allocation of pay between regular and overtime hours. If you don't, then in a wage and hour dispute, you might be ordered to pay back pay at an hourly rate that's artificially high based on the inclusion of those overtime hours.

CAUTION
If you offer a fixed paycheck, it's not fair to change your plans. Many parents wrongly assume it's okay to tell their nanny, "Don't come in this week. I don't need you and don't want to pay you." Technically speaking, this doesn't violate any laws (because your nanny is paid by the hour, even if you've set a fixed schedule of hours of pay), but it's considered seriously tacky. A better approach is to negotiate in advance how many weeks out of the year you'll pay the nanny, and then stick with that, regardless of the occasional times that you really don't need her to be there. Of course, you can negotiate a separate agreement on short notice, but your nanny may not be thrilled about it. And when planning vacations, you can ask that some of hers coincide with yours.

Paying based on hours actually worked might be better for you, however, if the times when you'll need the nanny are unpredictable—for example, you're self-employed but have to leave the house whenever you have a client appointment. Otherwise, you could end up paying for a lot of hours that the nanny doesn't work. To make this more palatable to the nannies you interview, you could offer a minimum number of guaranteed paid hours per month. And to compensate the nanny for those times when her hours are slim, you may have to pay a premium hourly wage for every hour.

Among British servants, who earns more than the nanny?

The butler, of course. And only the butler.

As far as which arrangement might lead you to overpay more often, there's no clear answer. Parents with troublesome nannies have reported that those paid fixed amounts tend to show up late and leave early; while those earning hourly wages show up early and create excuses to stay late! The key is to find a great nanny who won't play this kind of game, and communicate your expectations clearly.

Researching Local Nanny Rates

You're probably already quizzing your local friends and neighbors on how much they pay their nannies. Keep it up—and perhaps add some detail to your questions, asking not only about the amount, but also questions drawn from "Factors That Affect a Nanny's Pay Rate," below.

Factors That Affect a Nanny's Pay Rate

Although market supply and demand help determine the range of nanny pay rates in a given area, those amounts are usually driven up or down for particular families by the following factors:

- the number of children the nanny is caring for
- whether the nanny is paid a set amount or are based on hours worked
- whether the schedule includes odd hours like evenings and weekends
- how long the family has had the nanny, and whether the current payment figure includes past raises
- whether the family is paying the nanny legally or under the table
- whether the family has promised or plans on giving future pay raises
- whether the family gives year-end or other bonuses
- whether the family pays for health insurance or other benefits and perks
- whether the job involves more than the average duties (for example, caring for a dog and doing housework), and
- how much, if any, vacation time the family pays for.

In fact, many parents deliberately set their starting pay a little low, while making clear to the nanny that they'll raise it if her performance is satisfactory over the first six months or year.

If you opt to use a nanny placement agency (described in Chapter 6), it will give you guidelines on how much its nannies expect to earn and the assumptions about raises and benefits upon which that amount is based. You can also contact various local nanny placement agencies for this information; some post the dollar figures online.

Also look at local flyers and online job boards (at Craigslist, for example) to see how much other parents are offering or how much job-hunting nannies are seeking. Not all will make this information public, but enough will. Again, look not only at the pay rate, but the job description.

Settling on a Pay Rate You're Comfortable With

After doing your research, you'll probably still have some room for decision making. For example, a quick scan of the Craigslist ads in early 2010 showed that in the Bay Area, the overwhelming majority of parents paid on a fixed rather than a per-hours-worked basis, offering amounts that worked out to between $10 and $40 per hour, though most fell within a $15 to $20 an hour range.

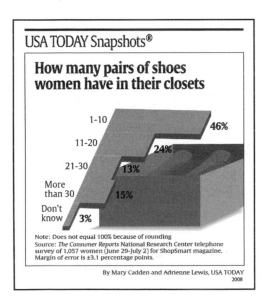

USA TODAY Snapshots®

How many pairs of shoes women have in their closets

1-10   46%
11-20   24%
21-30   13%
More than 30   15%
Don't know   3%

Note: Does not equal 100% because of rounding
Source: *The Consumer Reports* National Research Center telephone survey of 1,057 women (June 29–July 2) for ShopSmart magazine. Margin of error is ±3.1 percentage points.

By Mary Cadden and Adrienne Lewis, USA TODAY
2008

It's worth noting both the extremes and the usual going rate. (The high end of the extremes is described under "Nannies to the CEOs," below.) Assuming your income doesn't happen to reach CEO levels, the extreme highs will tell you that you might not be able to attract Mary Poppins with a Ph.D. in child development. But the normal pay amount will tell you how much most families are offering—an indicator that, if you can match that amount, you will find a fine nanny.

There's no need to arrive at a precise dollar figure before starting to interview candidates. Settle on your own range of what to offer, depending on the nanny's qualifications and experience—as well as what she earned at her last employer, which she'll very likely expect you to match or exceed.

If you can afford more than bargain rates, that's what you should pay—and not merely for moral reasons. It's no fun trying to hide your grocery receipts or sneak a new pair of shoes past the nanny, who will very quickly realize that your lifestyle doesn't match up to your claims of impoverishment. On the other hand, if you stretch too far in setting the level of pay, you may end up resenting the nanny and trying to get extra work out of her or shortchanging her on bonuses and perks.

With any luck, you'll arrive at a pay level that's both okay for your budget and will attract a nanny with whom you'll be satisfied. If the numbers still aren't quite coming together, consider offering a particularly good package of benefits, as discussed below.

> **CAUTION**
> **Your pay rate will dictate your overtime rate.** Did we say overtime? That's right, federal law says you owe one and a half times the nanny's usual hourly rate for any week in which she works more than 40 hours (even if she's on an otherwise fixed level of pay). Some states' laws (such as those in California, Alaska, and Nevada) additionally require you to pay overtime on any day that the nanny works more than a certain number of hours, usually eight (but 12 in Colorado). That means that you can't, in such states, work the nanny for ten hours on four days, then stop for the week and deny her overtime because you've kept within the federal 40-hour limit. You'll owe her overtime for the two extra hours on the ten-hour days. Good news if you're hiring a live-in nanny: These overtime laws won't apply.

Nannies to the CEOs

A single employee's resignation disrupted the life of Boston Beer Chairman Jim Koch.

It wasn't the CEO. It wasn't the chief financial officer. Rather, it was the nanny of his daughters, ages eight and ten.

Millions of families face upheaval caused by child care issues. CEOs are no exception. They are not insulated from a nanny gone sour, and their combination of anxiety and wealth is driving annual salaries of the best-paid nannies toward $100,000.

"There are people in Boston with JDs (law degrees) who make less than some nannies," Koch says. "We always looked at it as our most important hiring decision," Koch said.

Salaries of top nannies aren't the only thing being driven by the CEO search. Those at the high end also get benefits, such as health insurance, meals at fine restaurants, country club passes, cars with free gasoline, education stipends, cell phones, working trips aboard corporate jets to places like Hawaii and personal trips compliments of the CEO's frequent-flier miles. All that, plus room and board in a mansion, can make leaving the profession a lifestyle decision.

CEO nannies are in such demand that they often get unsolicited offers like a scene out of "Desperate Housewives." Angela Rheingans, 28, has been with the same Milwaukee family for eight years, but is often approached by strangers in parks and has found notes slipped under her windshield wiper at the children's school offering "to double whatever I'm making."

But Rheingans says she is bound by a sense of professional loyalty, not to mention three and a half weeks of paid vacation and a new Nissan Frontier four-wheel drive—although she says she gets to keep the truck even if she resigns tomorrow.

"I'm always approached. I have three standing offers," says Ingrid Hale, 37, nanny to the daughters, aged 21 months and 3 years, of David Gochman, CEO of Academy Sports & Outdoors, a Katy, Texas-based

Nannies to the CEOs, (cont'd)

retail chain that has more than $1 billion in revenue. Hale, who has 14 years of experience, makes $60,000-plus working 7:30 a.m. to 1:30 p.m. She figures she could top $80,000 with a typical schedule.

Why are high-end nannies so special? It starts with education. CEOs want college-educated nannies with degrees in such fields as education, nursing, and child psychology and are willing to pay for it, says Katherine Robinson, founder of Beacon Hill Nannies in Boston, which places 300 to 500 high-end nannies a year.

In addition to college degrees, many high-end nannies know how to swim, are certified in CPR, and regularly attend nanny seminars to hone their skills. Most at the high end have been through exhaustive background checks and psychological exams.

Movie stars such as Angelina Jolie, mother of a newborn, may be the most famous employers of nannies. But celebrities often prefer nannies who don't speak English because they don't want bathrobe secrets leaking to the *National Enquirer*, says Michelle LaRowe, who makes $80,000 a year working for a CEO in Boston.

LaRowe says she has talked to celebrities and the nannies of celebrities. She says that celebrities will brag to each other about how little they pay their nannies. CEOs brag about their nannies' qualifications. CEOs manage people for a living, pay the best, and are "fabulous to work for," LaRowe says.

Still, in the best neighborhoods, there are many nannies, typically uneducated immigrants, working for substandard wages, says Pat Cascio, president of the International Nanny Association.

But fewer CEOs take the inexpensive road because they are more sensitive to legal and tax issues and understand the risk of being sued for exposing unsuspecting young women to a "harsh work environment," says Joe Keeley, who is franchising a company of nanny agencies in major cities called College Nannies & Tutors.

> ### Nannies to the CEOs, (cont'd)
>
> Most nannies to CEOs sign confidentiality agreements never to discuss their families in detail. Those interviewed requested permission to speak to USA TODAY, including Myrna Alphonse, 34.
>
> She manages the housekeeper, lawn crew, and personal chef. "They saw the value," says Alphonse, who makes $70,000 a year, plus health insurance, paid vacation, sick days, and an education stipend that she is using toward her master's degree.
>
> Being a high-end nanny is not an easy life. Sixty-hour weeks are typical, and nannies often must work on Christmas and Thanksgiving.
>
> "CEOs shell out nearly 6 figures to secure the perfect nanny," by Del Jones, June 30, 2006.

Planning Ahead: Raises and Bonuses

After scraping together enough cash to pay a nanny at all, the last thing you may want to think about is paying her more in a mere six to 12 months. But every employee at least hopes for a regular raise—usually at the same time as the performance review. And you'll probably want to do a formal review after six months, so this is another issue to discuss at the outset with the nanny you hire.

If you're truly paying your nanny all you can, but want to be able to give her some incentive toward good performance, you might actually lower your intended pay a notch for the first six months, making clear that you'll raise it by a certain amount if she meets your expectations. Or you could create an alternate bonus for the six-month review, such as a paid day off or a gift certificate to a spa or masseuse.

After a whole year, professional nannies have normally come to expect a raise of between 5% and 10%—though these expectations went down in the recent recession, when parents weren't receiving raises, either. Even 2.5% is considered a respectable amount.

If you don't expect to be able to pay any raise at all, or if it's contingent on your own pay raise, make that clear in advance. An otherwise-satisfied nanny may well be content to stay on at the current rate. Again, however, think of other ways to compensate her for good performance, such as extra paid vacation or other perks—and a bonus. Amy, a mom in Seattle, says "We gave our nanny only modest raises over the five years that she was with us, but we did pay for her health insurance—and those rates kept getting hiked up significantly. So we continued to pay it with the understanding that it was similar to a raise."

USA TODAY Snapshots®

Most expect 3% to 5% pay raise
How much of a salary increase do you expect to get after your next review?

0% to 2%	20%
3% to 5%	60%
6% to 10%	16%
11% to 20%	3%
More than 20%	1%

Source: IABC survey of 3,370 workers. Weighted to actual population proportion.

By Jae Yang and Robert W. Ahrens, USA TODAY 2007

About that bonus. Have you read *The Nanny Diaries* yet? It's a fun read, and should perhaps be required of every parent. There's an unforgettable scene where the nanny, after a year of caring for a little boy in the face of dysfunctional family behavior of epic proportions, and knowing that the other family servants received cash gifts, opens her holiday gift to find . . . earmuffs. She's still talking about it several chapters later. Your nanny might have the same reaction if your gift doesn't feel equal to everything you've asked of her.

In fact, many parents give a week's pay as a bonus, usually in an envelope, in cash—(technically taxable, but parents hope the IRS won't find out). Very generous (or wealthy) parents have been known to give up to a month's pay.

But you can get creative and substitute or augment your cash bonus with other perks. Perhaps a weekend at your family's jointly owned vacation cottage? Or, gifts of your own services work nicely: For example, a dentist might give free dental exams; an engineer might buy a laptop (at company rates) and provide software and training; a lawyer might give advice on handling legal issues such as immigration;

a teacher might offer the nanny's children some tutoring or help on college applications; a car mechanic might offer discounted rates on work he'll do in his shop; and so on. Also, a handmade gift from the children is traditional, reflecting the fact that your nanny really has become more than just an employee.

> **TIP**
> **A simple "Thank you" goes a long way.** Over and over, experienced nannies will say how much it means to them to hear that the families value their hard work and their good relationship with the children. And if you really would have liked to give the nanny a bigger bonus, but your own employment situation prevented that, it's better to tell her than to ignore the issue. So long as you're being honest about your finances (which she'll probably be able to tell by looking at your spending habits), she's likely to understand. See Chapter 11 for more tips on making a good nanny feel appreciated.

Creating a Package of Benefits

To sweeten the deal, we'll next discuss the various benefits that you might offer your nanny. You'll be glad to hear that many of these won't involve any additional outlay of cash.

Vacation

Everyone needs a vacation once in awhile—and given the rigors of child care, especially if it's full time, your nanny may need a vacation more than the average person. Of course, she may get some random days off when you don't need her, but that's different from a vacation she can plan ahead for—and be paid for.

Is vacation for your nanny legally required? No, but it's expected. At least a few paid days off will help you avoid looking like a Scrooge. Five to ten days is typical. A generous number of vacation days can help compensate for a low rate of pay. (That vacation period might be a good time for a doting Grandma to visit!)

Some nannies may wish to take even more vacation, unpaid. For example, Shelley, from Virginia, says, "Our nanny was from Haiti, and she went back to visit a couple of times while she was with us. Because it was such a huge expense for her to go there, she wanted to stay for a really long time. I think she went once for three weeks, which was difficult for us to time with our work. But we dealt with it."

Make clear in advance whether you're open to such arrangements, or whether you really will need the nanny for every day of the year minus the allotted leave days.

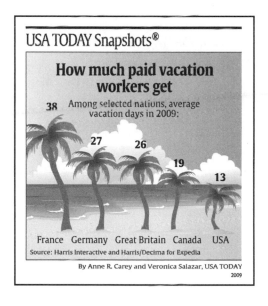

USA TODAY Snapshots®

How much paid vacation workers get

Among selected nations, average vacation days in 2009:

France 38
Germany 27
Great Britain 26
Canada 19
USA 13

Source: Harris Interactive and Harris/Decima for Expedia

By Anne R. Carey and Veronica Salazar, USA TODAY 2009

> ⓘ **CAUTION**
> **Be clear that you're paying only the usual amount while the nanny is on vacation, not for the vacation itself!** As Marilyn, a mom in Kalamazoo, Michigan, tells it, "Our nanny's English wasn't that great, and she somehow interpreted 'paid vacation' to mean we'd pay her plane fare and other expenses. I was horrified when she presented me with the receipts, and she was, of course, very disappointed to find out that wasn't the deal."

You can, if you like, insist that your nanny's vacation be scheduled so that it occurs at the same time as your own. But sometimes, this is difficult to work out. If you're offering ten days, you might compromise by saying at least one of the weeks must coincide. If the nanny can completely choose her own vacation times, you can require her to give you a certain number of weeks' notice before taking off.

Also consider whether you want the nanny to accrue the allotted vacation over time (like most employers require). That would mean that, instead of being able to take five days off after, say, six weeks of work, she would earn her vacation days month by month. If, for example, you offer five days of paid vacation per year, then the nanny would accrue that at a rate of 3.3 hours per month. (Here's the math: 5 days x 8 hours per day = 40 vacation hours per year, divided by twelve months = 3.3 hours per month.) Or you could go with the simpler and widely used method of saying she can use the five days as soon as she's been with you six months.

Sick Leave

You don't want your nanny dragging herself to work when she's sick. Even when she's not contagious (or your whole family has already had the bug), she probably won't be at her best in handling your children. For basic humanitarian reasons, many parents offer nannies sick leave. Between two and five days per year is common.

If the nanny ends up needing more sick days than that during a year, you can require that she take the remaining days out of her vacation leave or simply go without pay for those days.

Would it help you for the nanny to send a substitute when she's sick? Not every nanny can offer this, of course, but some have a friend or family member who can step in. The nanny can pay her out of her own wage, which would help the nanny if she's low on remaining sick leave. This is another topic you should discuss ahead of time. Plan to meet the proposed substitute before the nanny gets sick.

Paid Time Off

Instead of offering separate vacation leave and sick leave, some parents simply offer a lump amount of "personal time off" (PTO). The nanny can then use her PTO days for any purpose she wishes—not just for vacation or sick time, but to attend to family emergencies, run errands, or for other reasons. But it's not a perfect solution. Some parents have found that nannies with PTO continue coming to work sick, saving up their time for a nice long vacation.

Mandatory Time Off

You may also be required by your state's law to give your nanny paid time off for certain civic duties, most likely voting or jury duty. Your state department of labor can tell you more.

Snow or Other Transportation Emergency Days

If you live in an area where snow, floods, or other acts of nature might make the roads unpassable, it's best to establish ahead of time how the nanny's pay will be affected. Because the weather isn't her fault, most experienced nannies will expect to receive their pay regardless. Of course, it's not your fault, either. You could settle on half pay, or let the nanny make up the time. You might also discuss with the nanny ahead of time whether she'd be willing to stay overnight at your house when a storm threatens.

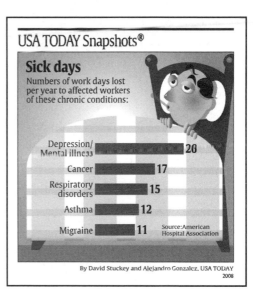

USA TODAY Snapshots®

Sick days

Numbers of work days lost per year to affected workers of these chronic conditions:

Condition	Days
Depression/Mental illness	20
Cancer	17
Respiratory disorders	15
Asthma	12
Migraine	11

Source: American Hospital Association

By David Stuckey and Alejandro Gonzalez, USA TODAY 2008

Paid Holidays

Another benefit that's not legally required, but is customary, is to give major U.S. holidays off with pay—particularly the "big four" holidays: Thanksgiving, Christmas Day, New Year's Day, and the Fourth of July. Ideally, you will have those days off from work, and can spend them at home with your children. Like any employer, you should provide in advance a list of the paid holidays you'll recognize, so that you aren't surprised when your nanny doesn't show up on Columbus Day.

Instead of just handing your nanny the list when she starts work, it's probably a good idea to talk it over with her. You may find that certain holidays are not that important to her; but that she might want to trade them for others. This might be the case, for example, if she observes religious holidays that haven't made it onto the list of standard work holidays.

Health Insurance

Most families don't provide health insurance benefits to their nannies, and doing so is not legally required under current law. Nor will it be required under the health insurance bill recently passed by Congress, due to exceptions made for small employers—though the nanny herself will be required to carry health insurance starting in 2014, assuming she's a U.S. citizen or legal resident.

> **TIP**
> **Major new health legislation had just been approved when this book went to print in April, 2010.** For how the new law plays out, keep your eyes on the news and on the Legal Updates provided at www.nolo.com. Also realize that many of the bills' provisions are not scheduled to take effect until as late as 2014, and delays are always possible.

There's no question that buying health insurance for your nanny would be a significant expense. (The exception would be a nanny who is already retired, in which case she will most likely be eligible for Medicare; or one who is under 26 who may, under the new law, remain covered by her parents' health insurance.) You probably won't be able to simply add the nanny to your family policy, because she's not actually part of the family. Instead, you'll have to research and purchase a separate policy, which tended to cost up to around $300 per month prior to health care reform. We can't predict how these costs will change as the health reform legislation takes effect.

The good news, however, is that the legislation contains tax credits of up to 35% of premiums for small employers that purchase health insurance for their employees (effective 2010) and will create state-based purchasing pools to make health insurance more affordable for small businesses. This will be a welcome change, because pre-reform tax laws didn't give you any direct tax benefits for paying an employee's premiums (though employers at least don't have to pay the type of taxes owed based on the nanny's paycheck, such as for Social Security, Medicare, and so forth).

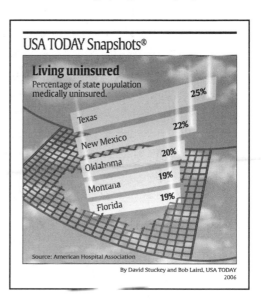

USA TODAY Snapshots®

Living uninsured
Percentage of state population medically uninsured.

	25%
Texas	
	22%
New Mexico	
	20%
Oklahoma	
	19%
Montana	
	19%
Florida	

Source: American Hospital Association

By David Stuckey and Bob Laird, USA TODAY
2006

In any case, the expense can ultimately pay off for you. First off, health insurance is a valuable benefit, which will help you attract a wider pool of applicants. Second, imagine the scenario if your nanny did contract a serious illness, such as cancer, and hadn't bought her own insurance. You and your children would face the trauma of watching her condition worsen until she couldn't work anymore or her income and assets fell to the point where she qualified for Medicaid. She might use up all of her sick days and then some before coming to the realization that she couldn't continue working. And you might feel duty bound to pitch in on her medical payments, perhaps ultimately wiping out any amount you saved by not providing insurance.

> **CAUTION**
> **An immigrant nanny may have very little backup.** For example, Evie, a mom in Albany, California, describes a tragic situation where "A former nanny of ours, who was originally from El Salvador, died unexpectedly. She had no other family in the United States, and there wasn't even enough money in her estate to fly her body home. We ended up pitching in with other parents whose children she'd cared for to cover the expense."

One compromise possibility (at least, prior to the changes brought about by health reform) is to provide what's called a temporary or short-term medical insurance policy (not available in all states). Unlike standard insurance, these insure a person for a specific length of time, such as one year. The policy covers most health costs during that time period, though it will probably exclude basic checkups and vaccinations. But once the policy expires, you have to start all over with a new policy. Any medical conditions that the insured person developed during the old policy become "preexisting conditions," which, until the anticipated health reform changes take effect, will be excluded from the new temporary policy's coverage. As a result, however, temporary policies cost much less than the standard ones, usually running around $75 to $100 per month.

Another compromise is to buy the nanny so-called catastrophic health insurance, which costs around $200 per month. True to their name, such policies cover medical expenses after a major accident or an illness that requires staying in an intensive care unit. If, however, your nanny's family budget is such that she can't set much money aside, such a policy can be problematic. It usually comes with a very high deductible, meaning that she'd have to pay the first several thousand dollars of medical expenses before the insurance kicked in. And, like the temporary policies, she wouldn't be covered for regular checkups, other preventive care, or simply everyday health problems.

If you're lucky, you might find a nanny who already has insurance through a spouse or parent (or, as mentioned earlier, Medicare). It's definitely worth asking her about. Perhaps you'll find that she could get coverage by simply paying a little extra on a spouse or parent's policy, in which case, you might offer to subsidize this. And if you're sharing a nanny, the expense to each family will go down.

If your nanny will be completely uninsured—which could still occur in the post-reform world, for example if you've hired an undocumented immigrant or someone who's paying the penalties rather than for actual health insurance—at least pay for her to get a flu shot (usually offered at local drugstores). This will serve everyone's interests in the long run.

Also consider paying for some basic preventive care, like a checkup and mammogram. Local nonprofit health organizations may offer these at low cost based on income.

> RESOURCE
> **For more information:** Talk to an insurance broker or go to a website like www.insure.com or www.esurance.com, which provide quick, anonymous price quotes.

Health Club and Other Memberships

It might not cost you much to add one more person to your health club, beach club, botanical garden, or zoo membership. Making your nanny a member will serve both your and her interests if it allows her to take the children for activities.

As Ellen, a former live-in nanny in New Hampshire, explains, "My favorite part of the day was taking the kids to the lake club. They could amuse themselves, and as long as I kept one eye on them, it allowed me to get in some much-needed time chilling out, reading, or talking to other adults."

Gas or Mileage Reimbursement

To lure a particularly good nanny, some parents have been known to reimburse her for mileage or other commuting expenses, especially if it's a long commute. This certainly isn't required, however. Of course, you should reimburse the nanny for transportation expenses that directly involve your children, such as driving them to classes or the park.

Entertainment Reimbursement

As with transportation reimbursement, you should cover the nanny's costs when she takes your children to the movies or buys them snacks during a walk or other outing. And that usually means covering the nanny's movie ticket or snack expenses, too. After all, if she's hungry but can't afford her own fresh-fruit smoothie, then she and your children are probably going to be eating fast-food French fries.

Naturally, this is an area where you'll want to set down very specific guidelines. Make clear, for example, how much the nanny can spend each week, what sort of field trips and food purchases are appropriate, and the extent to which you'd expect the nanny to simply pack a lunch or snacks. While some parents simply put out a jar of petty cash, others prefer to reimburse the nanny based on receipts.

USA TODAY Snapshots®

Want fries with that? Heck, yeah!
Fueled by the popularity of fast-food fries, consumption of frozen potatoes has boomed. Per capita consumption in pounds per year[1]:

17.48

9.12

1970   2005

1 – Per capita availability adjusted for loss due to processing and waste from farm to table

Source: U.S. Department of Agriculture/Economic Research Service

By Tracey Wong Briggs and Veronica Salazar, USA TODAY 2007

⚠ **CAUTION**
Junk food is a big area of contention between parents and nannies. Samantha in Charlotte, North Carolina, for example, says "I'd given our nanny strict instructions not to buy the kids any junk food. But then we'd be in a convenience store, and my daughter would point to some chips or something, and say 'Those are good!' When I'd ask her how she knew that, she'd say, 'The nanny bought me some, but she told me not to tell you.' Our nanny was otherwise wonderful with the kids, and took care of lots of household chores, but this one thing drove me crazy."

"I Need to Fill Out a What?" Tax, Immigration, and Payroll

In the past, most of the household help you've hired—whether it was the occasional painter, electrician, or gardener—were not, legally speaking, your employees. That's because they worked for other people besides you, supplied their own tools (and sometimes their own employees), and performed the work without your constant supervision and direction. In the eyes of the law, these workers were considered independent contractors. However, your relationship to your nanny is different. You are now an employer, and the nanny is your employee.

SKIP AHEAD
Hiring an international au pair? You can skip most of this chapter—except the sections called "Logistics of Paying Your Nanny or Au Pair," "Coverage on Your Auto Insurance," "Paying With Pretax Income: Dependent Care Accounts," and "Getting Money Back: The Child Care Tax Credit," below. In very rare situations, typically where they have hired au pairs without going through an authorized agency, people must also deal with the tax obligations described below. Assuming, however, that you hire your au pair through an authorized agency, there should be no need to worry. Ask your agency or tax adviser for more information.

Being an employer comes with a fairly defined set of responsibilities, including:

- checking your nanny's immigration status
- delivering regular paychecks
- withholding and paying the appropriate Social Security, Medicare, and other taxes
- getting an employer identification number, and
- paying for workers' compensation insurance.

We'll introduce you to the basics of how to do all these things in this chapter. However, as a busy and probably sleep-deprived parent, your best bet may be to hire someone else for certain of these tasks.

Why Nannies Can't Be Independent Contractors

It would be so much easier if your nanny could be classified as an independent contractor, in which case, you could pay her the same way you would a house painter—a straight sum, from which she'd pay her own Social Security and other taxes. But it won't work, which doesn't stop some accountants from giving parents risky advice to treat their nannies as independent contractors!

When you apply the IRS guidelines to the job done by most nannies, it's clear that they're to be considered employees. Here's how the IRS explains it: "The worker is your employee if you can control not only what work is done, but how it is done. If the worker is your employee, it does not matter whether the work is full time or part time or that you hired the worker through an agency or from a list provided by an agency or association. It also does not matter whether you pay the worker on an hourly, daily, or weekly basis, or by the job.

EXAMPLE: You pay Betty Shore to babysit your child and do light housework 4 days a week in your home. Betty follows your specific instructions about household and child care duties. You provide the household equipment and supplies that Betty needs to do her work. Betty is your household employee." (From IRS Publication 926, *Household Employer's Tax Guide.*)

Independent contractors, by contrast, are workers who do as many as possible of the following:

- earn a profit or suffer a loss from the work
- furnish the tools and materials needed to do the work
- are paid by the job, not by the hour
- work for more than one place at a time
- invest in equipment and facilities
- pay their own business and traveling expenses
- hire and pay any assistants, and
- set their own working hours.

Why Nannies Can't Be Independent Contractors, (cont'd)
Your state tax, unemployment, or worker's compensation agencies may have different ways of making this determination; you'll have to contact them to find out.
For a more personalized analysis, talk to an experienced accountant or tax lawyer. It's worth getting right: Otherwise, you could end up owing back taxes on your own behalf, plus the amount you were supposed to have withheld from your nanny's salary, plus penalties and interest. The total can add up to many thousands of dollars.

Verifying Your Nanny's Immigration Status

U.S. immigration law requires that you hire only nannies who have a legal right to both live and work in the United States. The fact that someone arrived in the United States legally does not mean he or she has a right to work here. For example, a tourist who comes from Europe may be in the United States legally, but the terms of a tourist visa do not allow him or her to work for pay.

Immigration law is highly complex, and no one expects you to learn it in detail. This section will give you some basic guidelines for verifying your prospective nanny's right to work and then explain the implications of hiring someone who is not allowed to work in the United States.

Checking Your Nanny's Immigration Documents

You'll have to verify that your nanny is legally authorized to work in the United States. No later than her first day of work, ask her to fill out U.S. Citizenship and Immigration Services (USCIS) Form I-9, *Employment Eligibility Verification*. It's available at www.uscis.gov (click "Forms," then look under "Most Searched Forms").

The form itself is fairly simple. We've reproduced a small version of the page that needs to be filled out below, so you'll get an idea of what it looks like.

You'll have to fill out the bottom portion of Form I-9 within three days after the nanny starts work, confirming that your nanny presented you with proof of her right to work in the United States. This can be somewhat confusing for employers, despite the lengthy instructions provided by USCIS. Here's a brief breakdown of the different ways that people can be authorized to work here and the documents that they're most likely to show you as proof:

- **U.S. citizenship.** All U.S. citizens are authorized to work, no matter how they obtained their citizenship. They might have become citizens by birth in the United States (in which case, they're likely to show you either a birth certificate or a U.S. passport); through their U.S. citizen parents or grandparents (in which case, they might present you with either a U.S. passport or what's called a "Consular Report of Birth Abroad"); or through a process called naturalization (in which case they're likely to show you either a naturalization certificate or a U.S. passport). Do not rely on a mere driver's license, which is not proof of U.S. citizenship. In fact, some states allow undocumented immigrants to get a license, and many allow immigrants who are here on a temporary visa to get one (by law, these visitors aren't allowed to work).

- **U.S. permanent residency.** New immigrants to the United States cannot become citizens right away. With a very few narrow exceptions, all must spend time as permanent residents first. In that case, they're likely to show you a photo identification card that says "Permanent Resident Card" or "Resident Alien" across the top. (These used to be green and were referred to as "green cards," but no longer.) If the immigrant is still waiting for the actual card to arrive by mail (which can take weeks or months after being approved for residence), he or she may show you a stamp in the passport with the code "I-551" on it.

- **Temporary visa with work privileges.** Certain categories of foreign-born people in the United States on short-term visas are allowed to work, at least until their permitted stay expires. In some (but not all) cases, their right to work is conditional on their applying for and receiving a work permit card (officially called an "Employment Authorization Document" or EAD). For example, the spouses of foreign diplomats or treaty traders or investors, the fiancés of U.S. citizens, and the spouses of exchange visitors may all apply for work permit cards. Such visitors will most likely present you with a photo ID card that says Employment Authorization Document across the top, or a Social Security card along with a photo ID such as a driver's license. Note that these EAD cards expire upon a stated date.

Sample Green Card

- **Other temporary status.** The categories of immigrants entitled to temporarily stay in the United States and work are too many to list here. For example, someone who has received refugee or political asylum status must wait at least one year before applying for a green card. Or, certain people permitted to stay in the United States until their home country recovers from a natural disaster or civil war receive what's called Temporary Protected Status. Fortunately, they routinely receive EAD cards.

Although we've listed the most likely documents you'll be shown, it's possible that your nanny will have different ones. For example, a U.S. citizen who has lost her birth certificate and hasn't applied for a recent passport might rightfully show you a combination of documents, such as a school photo ID plus a Social Security card. For a list of the acceptable possibilities, see the instructions that come with Form I-9. If you're still confused, ask the nanny whether she had help from an attorney, and ask her to ask the attorney to call you with clarification.

You won't have to submit your filled out I-9 to anyone. But you will have to keep it on hand in case you are audited. Nor do you need to photocopy the documents you're shown, although you can if you want to, for your records.

If a document your nanny shows you has an expiration date, you are legally responsible for asking her for new proof of her right to work upon that date. You'll have to fill in a new Form I-9, as well. For both your and the nanny's sake, mark not only that date on your calendar, but a date four months in advance, to warn her. She may need that time in order to apply for and receive a renewed work permit.

Form I-9

> ⚠ CAUTION
>
> **What if the nanny's documents are fraudulent?** Fake green cards, work permits, and other documents can be bought in the United States for a few hundred dollars apiece. If you are presented with an obvious fraud—such as a work permit with a new photo pasted over the plastic—you are legally bound to reject it. But many frauds are quite sophisticated, and it's not your job to become a detective and distinguish the good from the bad.

What Happens If You Hire an Undocumented Immigrant

Child care is one of the most obvious and available forms of income for undocumented immigrants (those without any legal right to be in the United States, sometimes called "illegal aliens"). And because the un-documented are usually willing to accept less money than people in the United States legally and to be paid under the table as well, many parents are willing or even eager to hire them. The practice is so widespread that people being considered for appointed political office routinely have to show proof that they won't have a "Nannygate" problem.

> ⚠ CAUTION
>
> **Hiring undocumented labor doesn't remove your obligation to pay employment taxes.** In fact, even without a Social Security number, the undocumented can apply for what's called a Taxpayer Identification Number (TIN) with which to file their taxes. If the immigrant ever becomes a legal resident, having paid taxes before becoming "legal" will help them establish their eligibility for Social Security later. In the meantime, the immigration authorities, being perpetually overworked, don't seem to use these filings to ferret out undocumented immigrants.

But even if you never plan on applying for political office, there are risks and potential complications to hiring undocumented help. The first question is, will you get caught? At the moment, the immigration authorities have their hands pretty full, and they're unlikely to come around looking for your nanny—even if someone tips them off. That's not to say it couldn't happen, in which case you might be fined several hundred dollars and your nanny would be arrested and removed. (And, by the way, immigration authorities have been known to leave children unattended in a home when arresting an immigrant.)

Sadly, you may meet some wonderful nanny applicants who are undocumented. Even if you want to do things right and help your nanny become a legal member of U.S. society, the laws make that exceedingly difficult. While there is a visa category that nannies could theoretically make use of—called "Employment Third Preference," or "EB-5," consisting of professional, skilled, as well as unskilled, workers—only 40,000 visas are allotted to this entire category every year. That means that even if all goes smoothly, your nanny could wait anywhere from three to ten years for a visa. In the meantime, her stay will continue to be illegal—and the fact that she stayed illegally could bar her from getting approved, at least within the next five to ten years. There have even been reports of immigration authorities following up on parents' filing of these the petitions for their nannies and arresting the nanny.

> ### When was the word "Nannygate" first coined?
>
> *In 1993, when Zoe Baird, Bill Clinton's first nominee for attorney general, failed to win confirmation because she'd hired undocumented immigrants to serve as both her chauffeur and her nanny, and failed to pay their Social Security and other taxes.*

 RESOURCE
Don't give up without consulting an immigration attorney. Immigration law is widely acknowledged to be more complex than the U.S. tax code, and you shouldn't make any final judgments about a nanny's immigration situation based on what you read here. Some undocumented immigrants may have options that only an attorney could figure out. An experienced immigration attorney will do a complete consultation for usually no more than $100. Contact the

American Immigration Lawyers Association (www.aila.org) for a list of attorneys in your area, or see Nolo's Lawyer Directory at www.nolo.com.

Withholding and Paying Taxes From Your Nanny's Salary

If you've ever received a salary, you probably noticed that your paycheck contained a lot of annoying deductions. Now that you're the employer, you're responsible for making those deductions. (And that's true even if your nanny is an undocumented immigrant.) We'll give you an overview of your responsibilities here, then direct you toward further resources for the details.

First, a little advance warning: Our ultimate recommendation will be that you hire a payroll service to handle all this. You'll probably see why as you continue reading; and the costs are relatively reasonable. As Tina, a mom in Washington, DC, who happens to also be a lawyer, explains: "I talked to some other parents, including one who teaches tax law. They all said, 'The system is so complicated, it's impossible to deal with on your own; plus, it's so easy to make a mistake; you're better off hiring a payroll service.' That's exactly what we did, and we were very happy with how easy it made things."

TIP

Sharing a nanny? You'll also need to share the tax responsibilities and compliance requirements, because each family is considered a separate employer. How much you owe will depend on what portion of her salary you're responsible for. Fortunately, you'll also be entitled to your proportional share of the valuable tax breaks described below.

What Happens If You Pay Under the Table

Even if you want to do things right, your nanny may not. Time and time again, we've heard from parents that the nannies they interviewed insisted on being paid in cash, under the table—so that they wouldn't have to pay taxes on their income.

Of course, such nannies may be shortchanging their own future if they ever hope to claim Social Security, Medicare, or unemployment benefits based on their past earnings. These benefits are worth an estimated $5 for every $1 put into the system. For these and other reasons, the nanny may change her mind later. For example, Chris, a parent in Texas, says, "After about a year, our nanny discovered that she couldn't get an auto loan or qualify for a home mortgage without a record of her income. So she asked to be paid legally after all."

USA TODAY Snapshots®

Two lengthy codes
Number of pages in:

King James Bible **1,472**

U.S. tax code **20,000**

Sources: Amazon.com and Internal Revenue Service

By David Stuckey and Adrienne Lewis, USA TODAY 2005

Paying under the table would certainly be easier for you; but unfortunately, it carries some risks. For example, if the IRS someday chooses to audit you (and it sometimes chooses its audit victims at random) and notices that your household has young children and parents working full time and you haven't been taking the child care tax credit, it may ask why not—and conclude that you've been paying a nanny under the table. You would then owe back taxes and penalties.

Similarly, if you lay your nanny off and she applies for unemployment benefits, the government agency may ask her, "Who was your employer?" The trail will soon lead back to you. Again, you may have to pay back taxes and penalties.

Another problem with paying under the table is that you won't be able to take advantage of dependent care accounts or the federal childcare tax credit—either of which is generous enough to offset much of the cost of paying legally. For more on the tax credit, see below, "Paying With Pretax Income: Dependent Care Accounts" and "Getting Money Back: The Child Care Tax Credit."

Finally, if you have any hope of ever qualifying for a federal job, having a nanny tax problem could wreck the deal. Maybe the possibility seems remote, but according to Tom Breedlove, of Breedlove & Associates (a household-employer payroll service based in Austin, Texas), "It happens. We've had more than one parent come to us who was being considered for a federal judgeship. In one case, we had to clean up the family's books going back ten years, and they owed plenty in back taxes and interest. We were at least able to convince the state tax authorities that, because the family was trying to do the right thing, they shouldn't be charged penalties or interest on top of the basic back-tax payments."

Nanny-Tax Evasion Widespread

Despite some high-profile cases of nanny-tax evasion, the tax is widely ignored. In 2003, the most recent year available, only about 241,000 taxpayers filed Schedule H, according to the IRS. The International Nanny Association estimates that about one million households employ nannies in the USA.

Families bypass the nanny tax for many reasons. Some are already struggling to pay for child care and can't afford it. Others employ undocumented workers. And some don't understand the rules, or think the tax is too complicated or burdensome, says Robert King, co-owner of Legally Nanny®, an Irvine, California-based company that helps people pay nanny taxes.

But this much is clear, King says: If the IRS audits your return and finds you have an off-the-books nanny, you'll owe back taxes and interest—along with penalties for tax evasion and fraud.

 "Did you pay all your taxes?" by Sandra Block, March 6, 2007.

Social Security and Medicare (FICA) Tax

Now let's turn to how to do things legally. Assuming you pay $1,700 per year or more to your nanny (or any worker), you'll need to contribute toward her Social Security and Medicare accounts (collectively referred to as FICA taxes, because they're based on the Federal Insurance Contributions Act). The idea is to help ensure that your nanny will have financial benefits and medical coverage when she retires. She is also expected to contribute a one-half share.

The total required contribution is 15.3% of your nanny's pay. So if you pay your nanny $10,000 a year, you and she will need to contribute a total of $1,530 in FICA taxes. Split between you and the nanny, that's $765 per year or 7.65% apiece. (Of that $765, $620 will be sent to Social Security and $145 to Medicare, but you won't need to handle this breakdown.)

In addition, your state may impose withholding requirements of its own. Your state tax agency can tell you more, or your payroll service if you hire one.

How does this work in practice? For starters, you'll need to withhold 7.65% of every paycheck (her one-half share). If you fail to withhold, you will become responsible for paying the entire 15.3% yourself.

When do you pay it? In theory, you might be able to wait until next April, when you'll simply attach IRS Schedule H, *Household Employment Taxes*, to your Form 1040. But because of the high amount you're likely to owe, that ends up not working for most parents. Tom Breedlove, of Breedlove and Associates, explains why:

"When you do your personal, federal income taxes at year's end, you have to be within the IRS's 'safe harbor.' In other words, you have to have already remitted at least 90% of what you owe or 110% of what you paid last year. If you haven't, the IRS can hit you with interest penalties. This is true for everyone, whether they've hired a nanny or not. For most taxpayers, their employer regularly withholds (and remits to the IRS) enough to bring them within the safe harbor, so they never need to think about this. Adding your nanny into the picture, however, creates a good chance that you'll end up having already paid say, only 85% of what you owe, pushing you out of the safe harbor."

The cleanest solution is to make quarterly estimated payments using IRS Form 1040ES. Although some parents try to get around this by asking their employer to withhold extra federal taxes from their regular paycheck, that can create other problems. For one thing, it won't help with your state taxes, which may be due on a quarterly basis. Also, Tom Breedlove points out, "If you terminate your nanny during the year, she won't be able to get unemployment benefits until you've paid up all your taxes. We offer to handle quarterly remittances for families who hire us, and don't charge extra for this. Most families appreciate staying caught up, especially when they realize they're being saved from accidentally spending the money."

Own a Small Business?
Don't Put Your Nanny on the Business Payroll

According to Tom Breedlove, "A lot of small-business owners, with the best of intentions, put their family nanny on the business payroll. They think it's a convenient way to sign her up for health benefits. Unfortunately, this is a huge mistake. What ends up happening is that, because the nanny is not a direct contributor to the business—and the IRS has been clear that she's not—including her wages with those of true employees means the company ends up taking an illegal tax deduction.

"We've seen several families who got themselves into trouble this way, and had to amend their personal and company tax returns for several years. I even heard of one situation where the nanny was diagnosed with cancer, and when the health insurance company found out she wasn't a legitimate employee, it refused all claims on the nanny, on the grounds that the company had committed health insurance fraud."

> **CAUTION**
> If you're *not* paying quarterly, don't spend the money you've withheld! You aren't required to actually set up a separate account for your nanny's withheld taxes—but you might consider doing so if you're not paying them quarterly. As Amy in Seattle found when she first hired a nanny, "I hadn't been smart enough to set the money aside, so it was a rude surprise the first time we realized how much we owed."

Unemployment Tax

If you pay your nanny $1,000 or more in any calendar quarter (any three-month period), you'll also have to pay federal unemployment (FUTA) taxes. Because this program is administered through state governments, and some states have their own unemployment tax, the total rate varies from state to state. However, the federal portion usually credits you for your state tax payments, after which the amount you owe usually comes out to a 0.8% of the first $7,000 of annual wages paid to your nanny. This, too, is paid with your April taxes and reported on Schedule H.

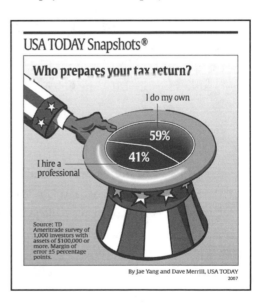

USA TODAY Snapshots®

Who prepares your tax return?

I do my own 59%

I hire a professional 41%

Source: TD Ameritrade survey of 1,000 investors with assets of $100,000 or more. Margin of error ±5 percentage points.

By Jae Yang and Dave Merrill, USA TODAY 2007

If you happen to have hired your or your spouse's parent or an underage child as your nanny you don't need to pay the FUTA.

Withholding Additional Tax at the Nanny's Request

As a household employee, your nanny is exempt from mandatory withholding of income taxes. However, there's a small chance she'll wish to have some money withheld. If so, by your nanny's first day of work, ask her to fill out IRS Form W-4, *Employee's Withholding Allowance Certificate*. (It's available at www.irs.gov.) This form will tell you how much she wants you to withhold and put toward her federal taxes.

Making Advance Payments for the Earned Income Tax Credit

If your nanny is a single parent, and her income is low enough to qualify her for the earned income tax credit (EIC), she may be eligible to receive advance payments from you. You'd include these in her paycheck throughout the year. Fortunately, you can reduce your Social Security, Medicare, and other tax withholding for her by the same amount.

Under certain circumstances, you're responsible for advising your nanny about her potential EIC eligibility. The safest thing to do is simply to hand her Copy B of Form W-2, which has a statement about the EIC on the back. Let her look into it and get back to you. If she qualifies for the EIC, she'll need to fill out, sign, and give you IRS Form W-5, *Earned Income Credit Advance Payment Certificate*.

> **RESOURCE**
> **For more information:** See IRS Publication 926, *Household Employer's Tax Guide*, and Publication 505, *Tax Withholding and Estimated Tax*, both available at www.irs.gov.

Preparing Form W-2

Another of your responsibilities as an employer is to prepare and file IRS Form W-2 at the end of the year. This is where you report the total amounts you paid to and withheld on behalf of your nanny over the year.

You can download Form W-2 from the IRS website, but this would require typing in the information by hand, and the form requires preparing multiple copies of the same information. An easier method is to visit the Social Security Administration (SSA)'s Employer W-2

Filing Instructions and Information website at www.socialsecurity.gov/ employer. The SSA lets you create the forms online, for free—and, in the case of the copy you'll need to file with the SSA, file it electronically.

Here's what you do with the copies:

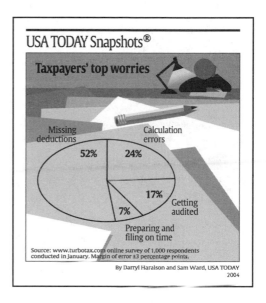

USA TODAY Snapshots®

Taxpayers' top worries

Missing deductions 52%

Calculation errors 24%

17% Getting audited

7%

Preparing and filing on time

Source: www.turbotax.com online survey of 1,000 respondents conducted in January. Margin of error ±3 percentage points.

By Darryl Haralson and Sam Ward, USA TODAY 2004

- Send Copy A with Form W-3, *Transmittal of Wage and Tax Statements*, to the Social Security Administration by its deadline (which is usually in early March, about six weeks before taxes are due, or late March if you file your Form W-2 with the SSA electronically)

- Give Copies B, C, and 2 to your employee by the deadline, usually February 1 of the year when taxes are due.

- Keep Copy D for your records.

Logistics of Paying Your Nanny or Au Pair

Now, to the matter of putting it all together and paying your nanny or au pair the correct amount on an appropriate schedule. The first question is how often you'll pay her. For au pairs, it's weekly. For nannies, your state's law may set a minimum—it may be as often as weekly (such as in California), though every two weeks is more common. Check with your state's labor board for details.

Paying most au pairs—that is, those who aren't subject to tax withholding—is fairly simple. You can give her cash, a personal check, or set up a bank account for her and make deposits directly into that, on whichever day of the week you agree on with her. We suggest, however, that you create a system of receipts, so that both you and she sign off on the weekly payment having been made. This helps prevent disputes resulting from short memories.

Paying nannies (and the rare au pairs subject to withholding) is more complicated. You'll need to set aside some time just before you owe a paycheck to calculate your nanny's hours—even if she's on a salary, given the possibility that she might have put in some overtime at your request. If she works hourly, set a time on which you and she check the time sheets or other records and agree on the hours worked.

Your overtime obligations are discussed in Chapter 4. Pay close attention to them, even if your nanny seems willing to let them slide and work extra hours for her usual pay. If your relationship changes, or the nanny simply gets tired of being paid for fewer hours than she works, she could take the matter to your state employment agency. There's no time limit on this—she could take action ten years down the line. And she's likely to win, in which case you'll owe her for all those unpaid overtime hours, plus interest and maybe penalties too.

Based on the total, figure out how much tax needs to be withheld. For an online calculator to help you, go to https://www.4nannytaxes.com/calculator/taxcalc (you'll need to register, but it's free). Keep a computer file or other written record of your calculations of the amounts paid and withheld.

Finally, you'll need to write the nanny a check and give it to her at the agreed-upon time. Some parents, as soon as they've written a check, put it in a regular spot—such as under the vase in the front hallway—for the nanny to find.

As we said, however, many parents find it far easier to hire a payroll service to handle paychecks for their nanny or au pair. Such services charge about $40 to $60 a month and take care of all the paperwork—calculating your nanny's tax withholdings, generating paychecks, preparing the nanny's W-2, and more. Among the services parents recommend are Breedlove and Associates (www.breedlove-online.com), PayCycle (www.paycycle.com), Nanny Tax, Inc. (www.nannytax.com), and 4NannyTaxes (www.4nannytaxes.com).

We asked Tom Breedlove, of Breedlove and Associates (which serves parents nationwide), to describe exactly how parents interact with a payroll service to get the check into the nanny's hands. He says, "When a client signs up with us, we get the standard payroll information, then build a private, password-protected Web portal for them. Immediately before each payday, we send a courtesy email reminder displaying the gross and net pay for the pay period along with a note saying, 'Here's what we're planning to process for payroll this pay period; if there are any changes, click here or call this number to modify your payroll.' If, for example, the employee took a half day off for personal reasons, the client would simply follow the link to the payroll module and change the hours from 40 to

> In every job that must be done, there is an element of fun. You find the fun, and SNAP the job's a game!
>
> **MARY POPPINS, IN THE 1964 MOVIE**

36. Voila, a new paystub appears in the window for review or approval. Once approved, the direct deposit is processed or the client can print the paystub and write their own paycheck. If the standard payroll was accurate, no action is required."

Getting an Employer Identification Number

Before hiring a nanny, you'll need to let the IRS know you're an employer, by getting a federal Employer Identification Number (EIN). You can do this via the IRS website at www.irs.gov (click "Businesses," then "Employer ID Numbers," then "Apply for an EIN Online").

Your state may also require you to get an identification number from its taxing authority and to register as a business. Check your state's government website for details. As with the federal system, your Social Security number alone won't suffice, because these tax ID numbers are used to identify you to government agencies that regulate employers.

Buying Insurance

There are three kinds of insurance you'll likely need to buy for your nanny:

- workers' compensation insurance
- state unemployment insurance, and
- if your nanny or au pair will be driving your car, coverage on your auto insurance policy.

We'll discuss all of these in this section.

Workers' Compensation Insurance Basics

What if your nanny gets injured on the job? As safe as your house might be, it's impossible to predict whether she'll catch her toe on a rug or cut herself with a kitchen knife. If the injury turns out to be major or disabling, the fact that it happened while she was working means that the nanny's own health insurance, if any, isn't likely to cover it. Your standard homeowners' insurance may or may not provide coverage, depending in part on your state's laws, as discussed below. There's a fair possibility that both will exclude such injuries with the expectation that you, as an employer, will have bought workers' compensation insurance.

The purpose of workers' compensation insurance is to not only provide medical care (including physical therapy) following an injury, but to replace a portion of the worker's income while off the job and then, in some cases, pay for rehabilitative care or job retraining. It also protects you from being held liable for the same expenses. In other words, your nanny has given up the right to sue you for injuries from work-related events in exchange for receiving benefits regardless of whether you were at fault in causing them.

Your state's law may, in fact, require you to carry workers' comp coverage. Some states exclude domestic employees, however, while some others say the rule applies only to employees who work a certain amount or employers of a minimum size. Contact your state's department of insurance for details.

If your state does NOT require you to carry such coverage and you own a home, there's a good chance that your homeowner's policy will actually cover the nanny's injuries in your home—in which case you won't need to buy separate insurance for in-home injuries. But check your policy to be sure. And realize that even the homeowners' policy won't cover the nanny for injuries that take place outside your home, for example if your nanny gets hit by a stray baseball while accompanying your kids at the playground.

USA TODAY Snapshots®

Workers' worth

Percentage of employers attributing certain traits to workers, by career stage:

Early | Mid | Late

Loyalty
22%
38%
54%

Creativity
35%
34%
22%

Source: The Urban Institute, 2006 data

By David Stuckey and Veronica Salazar, USA TODAY 2008

If you're required by state law to buy workers' compensation insurance, you may be able to do so through your homeowner's insurance policy, as a rider, endorsement, or as part of an umbrella policy. Or your state may offer a policy you can buy. Contact a local insurance broker for details.

State Unemployment Insurance Basics

Depending on your state, you will probably have to pay for state unemployment insurance for your nanny. This provides income replacement and other work placement services if you end the employment relationship and your nanny is unemployed. The cost of this insurance varies by state. Contact your state employment agency for more information.

Books to Help Your Kids Understand What a Nanny Is!

As long as you're studying up on what's involved in hiring a nanny, let your children do a little studying too! Okay, it's not exactly studying. But here are some children's books to help kids understand this new person in their home:

- *A Babysitter for Billy Bear*, by Miriam Moss (Dial, 2008). The first night that Billy Bear has a babysitter, she helps him overcome his fear that his mother won't find her way home in the dark.
- *My New Baby-Sitter*, by Christine Loomis (Morrow Junior Books, 1991). A straightforward nonfiction explanation of what children can expect from their nannies, and how this new relationship compares to that with their parents. Lots of photos.
- *Shirley's Wonderful Baby*, by Valiska Gregory (HarperCollins, 2002). Big sister Shirley the hippo learns to cope with both a new baby brother (whom she wishes would go back where he came from) and a new sitter.
- *Shoes Like Miss Alice's*, by Angela Johnson (Scholastic, 1995). A gentle account of a little girl's first day with a nanny, who teaches her to dance to the radio.

Coverage on Your Auto Insurance

If you plan to have your nanny or au pair drive your car, with or without your children, make sure your auto insurance policy allows for this. Start by reading your contract—but realize that if the nanny uses your car on a regular basis, she's no longer an "occasional driver," which all policies will cover. Then follow up with your policy representative.

Having your nanny added to the policy as an "additional driver" should probably be a simple matter, assuming she has a good driving record. Your insurer will probably ask for the nanny's name, date of birth, and driver's license number, in order to check whether she's gotten any past tickets. If you've hired an au pair with an international driver's license, she may have to also get a U.S. driver's license in order to satisfy your insurance carrier.

Paying With Pretax Income: Dependent Care Accounts

Now let's look at how to lessen the hit of all these tax obligations. If both you and your spouse or partner work, your first stop should be at one of your employers' human resources department, to ask whether it offers a dependent care account (also sometimes called a dependent care flexible spending account or a cafeteria plan). Similar to medical cafeteria plans, these let you set aside pretax dollars from your paycheck. After you've paid for the child care (whether from a nanny, an au pair, or another provider), you submit your receipts and reclaim your money.

> TIP
> **Your set-asides don't have to keep pace with your requests for reimbursement.** Although your employer will take the same amount out of each paycheck to put into your dependent care account, you can claim your reimbursements as soon as you've incurred them— you could request a whole $5,000 in January if you had the receipts to back it up.

A wide range of expenses can qualify for reimbursement under this account. If you have a regular nanny, you can get reimbursement for her wages and fees paid to a nanny locator agency. For a live-in nanny, you can claim any extra expenses for her room and board, though if your house had an extra bedroom anyway, no go—though you can still claim for utilities.

For an au pair, you can claim reimbursement for her wages, health insurance, extra expenses for room and board, and agency fees—but not for her airfare, visa, or school tuition fees.

There are some restrictions on whether your household qualifies, however. The first is that if you've got one stay-at-home parent in the household, even the working parent can't sign up for this type of plan. And the expenses must specifically allow you to work—money you pay to evening baby-sitters while you're at a concert or at dinner won't qualify. Also, care for kids who are 13 and over doesn't qualify.

The maximum amount that federal law lets you put into your account is $5,000 per household, regardless of the number of children or of whether you're single or married filing jointly. However, that limit gets halved to $2,500 if you're married filing separately. Your employer may, however, set a lower amount.

Do your research before choosing the amount. If you don't spend it by the end of the year, you will, in most cases, lose it. Fortunately, this ends up happening to only a small minority of parents. But if you do spend it, you may come out so far ahead that you actually save money by having paid your nanny legally.

> **RESOURCE**
> **For more information on dependent care accounts:** Talk to your employer's human resources department, in particular to obtain details on what expenses qualify. Also see the instructions to IRS Form 2441, *Child and Dependent Care Expenses*, available at www.irs.gov.

Getting Money Back: The Child Care Tax Credit

If you don't have access to a dependent care account, there's another option: Parents who are paying for a nanny, preschool, or day care while they work may be eligible for a federal tax credit—that is, a dollar-for-dollar reduction of their federal tax bill. It's good for up to 20% to 35% (depending on your income) of your first $3,000 in child care costs over the year.

Unfortunately, you can't have the IRS send you a check for any unused part of your offset—you can apply it only against the tax amount you were owed in the first place. Nevertheless, many parents find the credit very helpful in defraying the expenses of legally paying a nanny or au pair. But it's typically not as beneficial as a dependent care account, so if you've got access to one of those, go for it. You can't use both in one tax year.

As with the dependent care account, the nanny or au pair's salary or wages aren't the only costs you can claim toward the credit. Any fees you paid to an agency during the tax year while searching for the nanny or au pair may also be counted. Employment taxes you've paid based on the nanny's income may also be claimed. And if your nanny is a live-in, you may add on her extra room and board costs. But you can't claim the nanny's costs of commuting to your house, nor an au pair's transportation or airfare, not even if you're reimbursing her for them.

Your first task is to make sure your children fit the criteria for the child care expense credit. Each child must:

- live with you for more than half the year, and
- be under age 13 when the care is given or be permanently and totally disabled.

Next, you must figure out whether your nanny qualifies. She must:

- not be paid under the table; in other words, you must be paying employment tax for her
- not be someone you claim as a dependent—so, for example, if your mother lives with you and provides child care, you can't pay her, claim her as a dependent, and claim the child care credit—and
- be doing child care, not other household services (at least, not for the money that you're requesting the credit to offset).

Finally, you must make sure your own situation qualifies you for the credit. You must:

- pay more than half the cost of keeping up a home in which you and your child live
- work outside the home full time or part time, or be a full-time student; and if you're married, the same must also be true for your spouse, and

- have paid for the child care in order to allow you to work, look for work, or go to school (in other words, you can't be a stay-at-home parent simply looking for a break in your daily routine).

RESOURCE
For more information on the child care expense credit: See IRS Publication 503, *Child and Dependent Care Expenses.*

Job Available!
Getting the Word Out

The Internet has, without a doubt, made the job of looking for a nanny much easier than it once was. Nevertheless, you'll want to cast a wide net in your search, using both online and offline resources. This chapter will give advice on how to search for a nanny through:

- word of mouth
- reading ads, online and off
- placing ads, and
- using a nanny agency.

> **SKIP AHEAD**
> **If you decide to hire an au pair from another country, you won't need to go through these steps.** Chapter 8 will explain how an au pair agency screens candidates and matches you up with prospective au pairs.

Tap Your Network: Finding a Nanny Through Word of Mouth

Parents who've found a nanny through recommendations from friends or other contacts often feel great peace of mind about their decision. The nanny is a known quantity who has proven herself among like-minded people.

Fortunately, as a new parent, it's not hard to make contact with other new parents, even beyond your immediate circle. After you've mentioned your search to your friends (including via your Facebook or other social networking page and neighborhood listserv), talk to other parents and nannies at the playground, your work colleagues, and staff at local children's stores.

It could get a little roundabout; for example, Shelly, a mom in Virginia, describes: "A friend of mine, who had her older child in the same day care as mine, had a wonderful nanny whom they adored. That

Is It Legal to Search for Nannies of a Certain Race, Gender, or Religion?

Many parents would prefer a female nanny or one who shares the same religion as the family—and they might post an ad saying so. Except in the case of race-based discrimination (which is always illegal), this is usually not a problem. The federal laws prohibiting employment discrimination based on gender (including pregnancy or parenthood), religion, national origin, disability, or age apply only to employers of a certain size, thus generally not to households.

The state where you live may, however, have its own antidiscrimination laws—and these may be stricter than federal laws.

Does this mean that you have to cast a wide net and take whatever nannies you get? No. As employment attorney Bob King (founder of Legally Nanny®, a household employment law firm in Irvine, California) notes, "You can usually chart a safe course and still find the nanny you want by watching your wording and avoiding direct references to any legally protected characteristic or practice. For example, I've heard of parents saying, 'I want a Mexican nanny.' Advertising for that might look like national-origin discrimination; but when you talk to the parents, it usually turns out that they're just interested in having their kids learn Spanish. So I'd simply advise them to say in their ad, 'Spanish-speaking nanny required,' which is a legitimate, nondiscriminatory job requirement."

What about gender-based discrimination? If you really want a female nanny, Bob King points out, "Most of the responses to your ads will be from women. If you want a male, just say in your ad, 'Male or female candidates are encouraged to apply.' That shows that you're treating job applicants equally under the law, but also signaling, 'I'm open to a guy.' A male nanny would read that and say, 'Hey, that sounds like a good possibility,' and you'll have perhaps found your ideal candidate."

nanny had made friends at the park with another nanny, whom my friend had witnessed caring for children. My friend learned that this nanny was looking for a job, because the mom in the family she was working for would be staying home more. Knowing that a person I knew and trusted had seen the nanny at work did it for me."

USA TODAY Snapshots®

Love that home cooking
Times per week parents cook at home:

Once	6%
2 times	9%
3 times	15%
4 times	11%
5 times	20%
6 times	17%
7 or more	17%
Never	5%

Source: Harris Interactive online survey for SuperTarget of 496 adults living with children under the age of 18, March 23-27. Margin of error, ±6.5 percentage points

By Mary Cadden and Adrienne Lewis, USA TODAY
2007

Nonprofit or government-funded organizations dedicated to helping parents find quality child care are good places to check. Examples include BANANAS in Oakland, California (www.bananasinc. org), Child Care Resources in King County, Washington (www.childcare.org), or Child Care Information Services of Philadelphia (www.philadelphiachildcare. org). While such organizations don't necessarily provide listings of job-seeking nannies (some are more focused on licensed daycare centers), their counselors may be able to direct you toward local resources.

If you'll be approaching other nannies at the playground or elsewhere, be sure not to give the impression that you're trying to steal a nanny away from her current job. But if you see one who's doing a good job, it's worth finding out whether she has friends to recommend. And who knows, her employer may be putting the children into daycare soon, and she may be looking for her next assignment.

Read All About It: Checking Ad Listings

Many job-hunting nannies place their own ads seeking employment. The first place to look for these is online, at sites such as Craigslist (under "community," click "childcare") or your local newspaper.

Also check print ads, for example in small, neighborhood newspapers, tacked onto bulletin boards at local grocery or toy stores, community centers, or college job boards. You'll start getting a pretty good idea of each prospective nanny's English-language ability right here!

In some cases, you'll find ads by parents trying to help their own nanny, whom they can no longer use. For example, Shelly in Virginia describes, "We'd told our nanny ahead of time that we wouldn't need her once our younger girl turned three, at which point we'd arranged to enroll her at the day care where I work. But our nanny didn't want to leave us and kept telling me to have more kids! As a way of thanking and supporting her, we helped her find a job in the neighborhood for a family that we know; and she's with them still."

Placing Your Own Ads

For an even broader search, you can post your own "Nanny wanted" ads. The same places where you've already looked for nannies' ads should work, such as local bulletin boards, newspapers, and websites. On Craigslist, for example, parents place ads in the childcare section and under "Jobs/general labor."

When putting up physical ad notices, think about the age and type of person you want to attract and where you're most likely to find them. If you'd prefer a young person for part-time work, local college bulletin boards might be a good bet. If you'd like a mature person who has raised children of her own, look for bulletin boards at local senior centers. Remember, some of these people might not ordinarily check

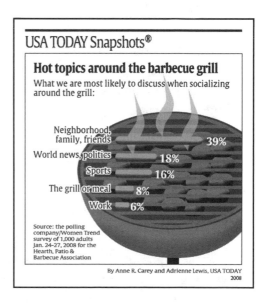

USA TODAY Snapshots®

Hot topics around the barbecue grill

What we are most likely to discuss when socializing around the grill:

Neighborhood, family, friends — 39%
World news, politics — 18%
Sports — 16%
The grill or meal — 8%
Work — 6%

Source: the polling company/Women Trend survey of 1,000 adults Jan. 24-27, 2008 for the Hearth, Patio & Barbecue Association

By Anne R. Carey and Adrienne Lewis, USA TODAY 2008

"help wanted" sites, but if an ad is right in front of them, they might think "Maybe this is a good way to spend my spare time and earn a little extra money."

College Student Nannies

Placing an ad on a college bulletin board might yield a good number of applicants. College kids are always on the lookout for additional income. Families looking for a nanny often assume that because students are young and not that far removed in age from their charges, they will be both energetic and able to bond easily with the kids.

While you may end up with a terrific college student nanny, realize that the assumptions mentioned above may not come true for every student applicant. Youth doesn't necessarily bestow the kind of patient, sustained energy that child care requires; and being close in age to the child does not guarantee the wisdom that good child caring requires (in fact, many college students are downright immature).

A student's life is anything but steady and predictable. There are papers to write, exams to study for, class schedules to keep—and schedules change two or three times a year. As Lizzie, a mom in Greenbrae, California, says, "The students were fun to be around, but their schedules were constantly changing—and they couldn't help it. We felt badly when our family needs interfered with their needs to study and attend class. We might have been better off with less interesting, but more dependable nannies."

The purpose of your ad is to attract applicants—but not every possible applicant. This is your first chance to do some early screening, warning away applicants who don't meet your criteria or wouldn't want the job anyway. Some good details to specify in your ad (as space allows) include:

- what area you live in

- start date

- something about your personal values or preferences about the nanny's approach (for example, one parent we know who was looking for part-time nanny mentioned in the ad that her children were at a Montessori school—with the result that the ad was answered by a fabulous ex-Montessori teacher!)

- the number and age of your children

- hours per week

- job responsibilities other than regular child care (such as cooking, light housework, and accompanying your family on vacations)

USA TODAY Snapshots®

Part-time job might make retirement better

Percentage of respondents who said retirement is better than expected because of:

34% Not working
45% Working part time
35% Working full time

Source: 2006 Merrill Lynch New Retirement Study of 2,189 respondents 65 and older. Margin of error ±1 percentage.

By Jae Yang and Keith Simmons, USA TODAY 2006

- salary (if you don't want to state the actual amount, but will be paying a regular salary, you can just say "salary")

- other benefits, such as health insurance or room and board

- English-language requirement

- state driver's license requirement, if any, plus whether nanny must provide her own car for driving your children

- nonsmoking requirement

- level of experience you're looking for

- references required

- any other requirements, such as age or gender, and

- how to contact you, and what application materials (such as a cover letter, résumé, list of references, or proof of a clean driving record) you might like to receive immediately.

Putting it all together, your ad might look something like this:

> Appleton single father looking for experienced, nurturing
> woman to provide care for two-year-old daughter and six-
> month old son, starting as soon as possible. Full time (40
> hours per week), plus occasional overnight stays while I'm
> away on business. Salary, health benefits, two weeks' annual
> vacation. Must speak English, have valid Georgia driver's license
> and clean driving record, and provide references. Experience
> with infants preferred. Am also hoping to find someone who
> enjoys reading aloud, singing, and taking kids to local parks.
> Nonsmokers only. Please send letter describing yourself,
> résumé, and references to singledad@email.com.

Hiring a Nanny Through an Agency

If you Google "hire a nanny," many of the first results to pop up will
be agencies offering to match you up with a nanny—at a price, of
course. The initial application fee may be in the range of $150, but the
placement fee (after you've chosen a nanny) is usually at least $2,000 or
a percentage of the nanny's first-year salary. Many parents find that it's
worth their time and effort to go without an agency.

However, if you're pressed for time and can afford the fee, hiring an
agency can shave a couple of weeks off the nanny-finding process (but
no more—remember, you still need to interview the candidates and
make your own decision, and you should independently check your
finalists' references). Here are the tasks that most good agencies will take
off your hands:

- advertising
- screening, including a criminal background check (which we
  advise that you do even if you don't use an agency, as discussed in
  Chapter 7)
- matching potential interviewees to your criteria, and

- helping set up your employment arrangement, including providing a standard form contract.

A few agencies also give the nannies on their list child care training, but not all. The agencies most likely to commit this level of resources are the ones at which nannies sign an exclusive representation agreement, meaning they promise not to sign up at any other agency. More commonly, the agencies allow the nannies they list to also put their names on other nonexclusive agency lists—which the nannies typically go ahead and do, along with continuing to scan the ads on their own. The upshot is that you shouldn't worry that hiring an agency is the only way to reach high-quality applicants.

Some parents start the advertising and interviewing process without an agency, figuring if they find a nanny on their own, great—and if they don't, they can always sign up with an agency.

If you're interested in an agency, start your search for local options at www.theapna. org, the website of the Alliance of Professional Nanny Agencies. It's a nonprofit that screens its member agencies to make sure they comply with professional standards. Another worthwhile directory is on the website of the International Nanny Association (INA), at www.nanny.org. Its member agencies must pledge to adhere to INA standards. You might also get referrals from friends and neighbors.

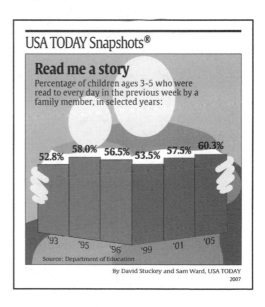

USA TODAY Snapshots®

Read me a story
Percentage of children ages 3-5 who were read to every day in the previous week by a family member, in selected years:

52.8%　58.0%　56.5%　53.5%　57.5%　60.3%

'93　'95　'96　'99　'01　'05

Source: Department of Education

By David Stuckey and Sam Ward, USA TODAY
2007

Once you've got a list of possibilities, it's time for some research. Using a combination of calling each agency, checking its website, and then scheduling a personal meeting at each place you haven't already eliminated, find out the following information:

- **The agency's history and record of success.** You want one that's been in business for a few years and placed at least a few hundred nannies. Also ask about what percentage of the placements have resulted in long-term employment relationships. A solid majority is good—but don't believe an agency that says "100%."

- **How much you'll pay and what the final amounts depend on.** You may have to pay both an application fee (probably a few hundred dollars) and a placement fee. Make sure the placement fee depends on your actually finding a nanny—and that you can get at least a partial refund if the nanny doesn't work out or leaves within a short time. In place of that, some agencies say they'll send a new nanny at no added charge. You'll have to decide whether that's okay with you, given that it places less responsibility on the agency to find you the best nanny from the start.

- **Whether you'll owe money even if you end up finding a nanny on your own.** If you find the perfect nanny through an ad or a friend, you shouldn't have to pay full freight at the agency.

- **Whether the nannies also pay fees to the agency.** Although it might seem natural for the nanny to pay a fee as well, usually upon being placed with a family, watch out for such arrangements. It can result in the agency being overly eager to place even the lowest-quality applicants, just to collect the fee.

- **The situations in which the agency will refuse to list a nanny.** You'll definitely want an agency that interviews each nanny in person and does comprehensive checks on the nanny's criminal background, employment record, and driving record. (If this isn't done before listing the nanny, at least make sure the agency follows through on the criminal and driving background check after you've expressed interest in hiring a certain one.) Some agencies also require the nannies to undergo a medical exam, show proof of eligibility to work in the United States, and meet other criteria, such as speaking English and having a minimum number of years of child care experience.

- **Whether the agency specializes.** For example, a few agencies represent nannies of only one ethnic group (a practice that may violate federal employment discrimination laws, but that no one seems to have made a case out of yet) or nannies trained to work with special-needs children.

- **Whether the agency trains its nannies.** A minority of agencies provide CPR or first aid training, while others simply require that the nannies on their list get this training on their own. Some agencies also prepare written materials for the nanny to review or use in the course of her work. Beyond that, there is no standard training that's required of nannies, although the International Nanny Association (www.nanny.org) has developed a list of resources and a recommended curriculum.

USA TODAY Snapshots®

Vacation more important for younger generation

Percentage who said taking a vacation is very important, by age:

Age 18 to 34 — 74%
35 to 54 — 66%
55 and older — 61%

Source: Access America and Ipsos Public Affairs survey of 1,000 adults 18 and older. Margin of error ±3 percentage points

By Jae Yang and Sam Ward, USA TODAY
2009

- **Whether the agency requires you to pay a minimum salary.** If so, and it's above what you're ready to pay, better keep looking. Even if the agency sets only a suggested salary range, if that's too high, you may have trouble getting a nanny from the agency to accept a lower salary.

- **How the agency will get to know your needs.** For maximum efficiency, find an agency that spends time with you—preferably in person—trying to get a good sense of what you need. Make sure they use this information to introduce you to suitable matches. If you're simply given a form to fill out or an online database to review, you'll spend a lot of needless time interviewing nannies who turn out to be not a good match.

- **How much help the agency will give you after you've chosen a nanny.** There's a fair amount of paperwork involved in extending an offer to the nanny and preparing an employment agreement with her. Look for an agency that will handle the bulk of this work on your behalf.

- **Whether the agency will advise you on tax and immigration matters.** Of course, you shouldn't rely on the agency as you would a lawyer or an accountant, but it should be able to answer basic questions on tax and immigration issues that arise when hiring a nanny.

- **What recourse you'll have after a mismatch.** If, within the first few months or some set guarantee period, you discover that the nanny wasn't what you thought, or the nanny leaves, the agency should arrange placement of a new nanny at no extra charge—and ideally refund some of your money.

- **What ongoing support the agency will provide your family.** Some agencies will call regularly to check in with you and the nanny, help out with miscommunications and disputes between you and your nanny, or arrange substitute child care if your nanny is sick or fails to show up for work.

- **What ongoing support the agency will provide the nanny.** For example, some will help nannies connect with other nannies in their area, host events, or alert them to opportunities for additional training or refresher classes. This can help the nanny feel professional and supported.

All of the above points should be clearly set out in a contract prepared by the agency that you review and sign. It's okay to request amendments to the agency's standard form contract, no matter how official and final it looks. These can be either written in the margins or attached as a separate document.

Summary of Questions to Ask Prospective Nanny Agencies

Here's a handy list to have at the ready when calling or meeting with the staff at a prospective nanny agency:

- Are you a member of the APNA or INA?
- How long have you been in business?
- What's your success rate in placing nannies with families? (And how do you define "success"?)
- Exactly how much will I need to pay?
- How is that payment amount affected by things like my being unable to locate a satisfactory nanny through you or finding a nanny who leaves or whom I fire within a particular period of time?
- Will I still owe you anything if I end up finding a nanny on my own?
- Must the nanny also pay you any fees?
- What screenings do you perform before placing a nanny on your list?
- Do your nannies have a minimum amount of education or experience?
- Do you specialize in any particular type of nanny (such as those with expertise working with children with disabilities)?
- Do you provide the nanny with any training classes or materials?
- Do you require or suggest a minimum salary?
- How will you get to know my needs regarding the nanny? Will you take them into account when proposing candidates for me?
- Once I've chosen a nanny, what kind of help will you give me on setting up the employment relationship?
- Will you provide me basic information and answer questions on tax and immigration matters?
- Will you provide follow-up assistance and placement if the nanny leaves or I have to fire her within a particular time period?
- What other ongoing support will you provide me?
- Will you arrange a substitute if my nanny gets sick or fails to show up for work one day?
- What other ongoing support will you provide the nanny?

You Meet at Last: Prescreening, Interviewing, and Background Checks

Finding a nanny you're comfortable with can seem as emotionally complicated as finding someone to marry. So much is happening at once: You want to make sure the applicant is not only qualified, but that you like her personally. You want her to like you well enough to choose your family over the others who may be competing for her services. Last but not least, you want to ferret out any clues that her stellar qualifications might all be a sham, created as a means to steal your possessions or molest your children.

First, let us say that there are many wonderful nannies out there, and that you *can* find one whom you're not only happy about, but delighted with—someone you'd trust to do the right thing in any situation. Nevertheless, one of the biggest mistakes parents make is to rush to the finish line. After what feels like a long, hard search, they meet an applicant who seems likable, and assume—no, hope—that the search is over. They ask some polite questions, are impressed by the list of references, and sign her up. In fact, they haven't really done their homework.

> **TIP**
> **This chapter applies mostly to the search for nannies, not au pairs.** As described in Chapter 8, your au pair agency will handle advertising and screening, and you won't get to meet the applicants in person. However, you might draw on the suggested interview questions in this chapter for conducting phone interviews with your prospective au pairs.

No one should skip the due diligence steps suggested here—even parents who are competent and vigilant people get conned. For example, Vivian, in Princeton, New Jersey, says, "We've had a number of nannies over the years, and by the time my oldest boy was 13, I thought we were old hands at the process. So I didn't think twice about planning to leave our latest nanny with the kids while my husband and I took a much-needed three-night vacation to St. Thomas. She had come through an agency. She had her own car, spoke good English (her native language was Romanian), and she cooked well. Before we left, I gave her some cash and sent her to Sam's Club to get food for while we were away. She came back, and I said, 'Where's the stuff?' She said it was still in the car, and that she'd unload it later. I should have followed up, but was rushing around preparing. I talked to her while we were in St. Thomas, and everything sounded fine. But then when we got to the airport to come home, she stopped answering her phone. I reached my oldest son when we landed in New Jersey, and he told me that the nanny wasn't there. She'd left my three kids—ages 13, 9, and 6—in the house alone. I asked him to go check for her stuff. It

USA TODAY Snapshots®

How many candidates must you interview to find one quality hire?

One	0.4%
2 to 3	24.4%
4 to 6	42.5%
7 to 10	20.0%
More than 10	12.8%

Percentages more than 100% due to rounding.
Source: Development Dimensions International Selection Forecast of human-resource professionals

By Darryl Haralson and Robert W. Ahrens, USA TODAY
2005

was all gone. She'd cleared out, having taken with her the grocery money, various items from the house, my credit and debit cards, and even food from the fridge."

What's the lesson here? It's not to mistrust everyone. That can only lead to shutting off the parts of your own intuition that help you make personal connections with others. Your intuition will be very important in this process, both to establish rapport and, on the flip side, to alert you to potential trouble.

Bizarrely enough, the lesson can be encapsulated by one of President Ronald Reagan's favorite expressions in dealing with the Russian government: "Trust, but verify." Whether you're dealing with nukes or nannies, the verification process will involve asking some tough, impolite questions and taking some probing investigative actions. But your role as the protector of your child gives you license to do these things. You'll soon discover that the good nannies won't mind, and that others will reveal themselves in surprising ways. And whatever you do, don't let yourself get rushed and let your guard down.

In this chapter, we'll lay out all the steps to take in screening and choosing a nanny, including how to:

- Weed out some applicants through effective prescreening.
- Conduct an interview where you and the nanny really talk.
- Verify the nanny's credentials through reference and background checks.

> **TIP**
> **Hang in there until you find the right nanny.** As Darius, a father in Alameda, California, tells it, "We went through a long day of interviewing nannies who just weren't right—a lot of young girls whom we could tell would be gone in a year. We were about to give up when finally, the very last interviewee was a 65-year-old woman, originally from Peru. She was very responsible and ready to teach our kids Spanish. She ended up staying with us for eight years. For the second four years, we asked her to live with us. We're still friends, and our kids are bilingual."

Prescreening Applicants by Phone

There's no need to personally interview every nanny whose ad you answer, or who answers your ad. It's more efficient to start with a phone conversation. This lets both of you learn about each other's requirements, expectations, and so forth. You may find very quickly that, for reasons that have nothing to do with the nanny's basic qualifications or individual goodness, she and your family are not a match. Or, if her level of English makes it difficult to communicate, you might decide this won't work out.

Avoiding Discrimination Issues During the Interview Process

As we discussed in Chapter 6, it's wise to simply avoid the possibility of discrimination lawsuits—and you can do so by paying attention to how you word your questions. Avoid making any direct inquiries about an applicant's race, color, gender (including pregnancy or parenthood), religion, national origin, disability, or age. It can be helpful to consider whether there's a deeper motivation for what you think you want.

For example, employment attorney Bob King, founder of Legally Nanny® in Irvine, California, explains: "When a parent is tempted to ask whether the nanny is pregnant or intends to get pregnant, what they really want to know is, 'Can you commit to a certain amount of time working here?' So it's best to ask the question in terms of the applicant's ability to commit to a certain amount of time.

"And instead of asking, 'How many kids do you have,' which could be interpreted as discrimination relating to family status, parents can say, 'Tell me about your child care experience,' which often will elicit the same information. Instead of asking about medical conditions, you can say, 'Here are the job requirements; can you meet these with or without reasonable accommodations?' or 'Can you walk up stairs?' rather than, 'Do you have any disabilities?' Most questions can be rephrased so that they pertain to legitimate job requirements."

It's probably better for you to take the lead in the conversation. Regardless of what the nanny may have already been told or read in your ad, start by telling her about your child, what the job involves (including scheduling and primary responsibilities), and what qualifications and experience you require of job applicants. Ask her whether she can meet those qualifications and is interested in the job as you've described it. (No need for detail yet, you'll go into all of this at your in-person interview.)

USA TODAY Snapshots®

Family chatters
Estimated number of people in the USA who speak languages other than English at home (in millions):

Spanish or Spanish Creole	29.7
Chinese	2.2
French	1.4
Tagalog[1]	1.3
German	1.1
Vietnamese	1.1

1 — Tagalog is an official language of the Philippines.
Source: Census Bureau

By David Stuckey and Sam Ward, USA TODAY
2006

Also ask, assuming you don't want to hire an undocumented person, whether the nanny is legally able to work in the United States. Don't ask this only of nannies with an accent. She could, after all, be a visiting Canadian who is violating immigration laws by working. (And in the worst-case scenario, your unequal treatment could lead to a discrimination claim.)

If there's something particularly important to you—for example, if you can't stand the smell of cigarette smoke and are adamantly opposed to hiring someone who smokes, even off the job—put that on the table now.

CAUTION
Smoking causes frequent conflicts between parents and nannies. Vivian, of Princeton, New Jersey, says, "I've had many tell me they didn't smoke when they did." Jackie, who lives in the Bay Area of California, says, "I knew that our nanny's parents smoked, so I hoped that was the reason she sometimes came in smelling like smoke. But then one day, my 2-½-year-old son picked up a Lincoln Log, put it in his mouth and pretended to smoke! I knew he'd never seen smoking among my family or friends, nor on the TV shows he was allowed to watch. So I had to confront the nanny and say, 'I want to reiterate, it's very important to me that you not smoke and not smoke in front of my kid.' She said, 'Of course, I understood that.' I'll never really know if she was smoking. But I didn't see my son trying to smoke his Lincoln Logs after that!"

Allow the nanny plenty of time to ask questions of you. She'll probably be curious about the pay. Most parents like to avoid discussing actual numbers at this point, unless they're offering an impressively high salary. You can explain that the exact amount will be worked out after you've had a chance to review your eventual hire's qualifications. That helps make sure that you don't close the door to someone who turns out, later in the interview process, to be so great that you're willing to pay a little extra or offer special perks to in order to woo her away from other families.

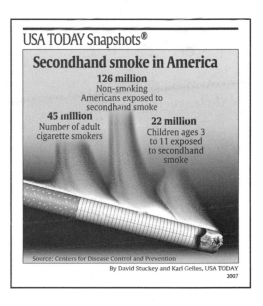

USA TODAY Snapshots®

Secondhand smoke in America

126 million
Non-smoking Americans exposed to secondhand smoke

45 million
Number of adult cigarette smokers

22 million
Children ages 3 to 11 exposed to secondhand smoke

Source: Centers for Disease Control and Prevention

By David Stuckey and Karl Gelles, USA TODAY
2007

In answering the prospective nanny's questions, you'll probably feel a bit like you're trying to sell her on your family. For example, if she asks something like, "Does your child cry a lot?" you may find yourself reassuring the applicant that your child is very easygoing. First, remember to be realistic—if your child really does cry a lot, and that's an issue for the nanny, better that she know about it now. But realize at the same time that you can learn a lot about her from such questions. You might follow up with a question of your own, such as, "Was crying a problem in prior households where you worked, and how did you deal with it?" Be wary if she starts telling you how horrible her previous employer or their bratty child was—there may be two sides to the story.

If both you and the nanny are still interested in one another, ask for any vital information that you haven't already received: her full name, address, contact information, and the names and numbers of the least two references, preferably former employers. Explain that you'll be reviewing this material and then contacting prospective nannies to schedule interviews.

If you're not interested—even if you're just not getting a good feeling about her over the phone—you can either gently tell her that you don't believe this is the right job for her or take down basic contact information and say that you will contact only the people you're interested in within a few days.

Make-or-Break Conversations: Reference Checks

Are we suggesting that you check prospective nannies' references even before you've held interviews or become seriously interested in hiring a particular one? Yes, you'll save time in the long run. It takes only about 20 minutes to talk with a reference on the phone, and if a prospective nanny's performance is described as less than stellar, that's an hour-long interview you can cross off your list.

> **Captain von Trapp** (*speaking to the new governess for his seven children*): *Fraulein, were you this much trouble at the abbey?*
>
> **Maria**: *Oh, much more, sir.*
>
> THE SOUND OF MUSIC, 1965

Before you call each reference, prepare a set of actual questions, using a combination of those on our list below and ones you come up with reflecting your own special concerns. Then get out a pad of paper and plan to take lots of notes. (You think you'll remember the details later, but you won't, honest.)

Note that we avoid yes or no questions, like "Was she a good employee?" Those won't elicit the kind of detail you want. Also, they make it too easy for someone who's reluctant to give a bad reference to be vague. Why wouldn't a parent be completely open about his or her experience with a nanny? A whole host of reasons: The person might feel guilty about having played a part in a bad working relationship, not want to damage the nanny's future, or not want to admit that their family allowed someone less than worthy to care for the children. In the worst-case scenario, you might be talking to a person who wasn't really the nanny's employer, but is just a friend doing her a rather large favor.

However, there's one situation in which yes or no questions are useful: That's in double-checking on whether the person providing the reference is, as we just mentioned, a fake. For example, if the nanny told you this family had three children, you might say, "And you're the family she mentioned who has two children, right?" Someone who's for real will correct you—someone who's not might just agree, in order to go along with what appears to be the nanny's latest story.

Assuming the reference passes that test, here are some more questions to ask:

- *When and for how long did the nanny work for you?* Her performance during a three-month stint five years ago carries weight only if the nanny is providing other, more recent references.

- *How did the relationship end?* If the nanny flaked out on the family despite having implied that she'd stay long term, or worse yet, was fired, ask for more detail.

- *What were the nanny's hours?* Reports on what she was like while working full time or as a live-in might be more relevant to your situation than if she simply watched the kids twice a week while the dad worked at home.

- *How much did you pay her, and was it on the books?* This will help you anticipate what the nanny expects by way of salary. (Also ask the nanny how much this family paid her—it's a good honesty test.)

- *What were her job responsibilities?* For example, ask how many kids she was caring for and what were their ages, whether the family shared her with another family, whether she did housework or meal preparation, whether she drove the kids to classes or took them on field trips, and so on.

- *How often did she call in sick?* And did she request additional leave time as well? Even if she wasn't abusing her sick leave, it's worth knowing if the nanny is in poor health or is dealing with personal circumstances requiring extra time off.

- *How did your child feel about the nanny?* As much as it irks some parents, if a child sometimes called the nanny "Mom," that's a good sign. The same is true if the family has kept in touch with the nanny for the sake of the child, perhaps still calling her or inviting her to birthday parties.

- *Did you like the nanny personally?* This is relevant—you'll be in a close relationship with the nanny, even if you cross paths only early and late in the day. And if she'll be living in your home, or working while another parent is in the home, it's extra important that she be easy to get along with.

- *Did you have to make any adjustments in order to communicate effectively with her?* Here's where you find out whether the nanny's English is up to par, and whether the parents had to accommodate difficult parts of her personality.

- *Can you give examples of situations where the nanny was trustworthy and reliable—or not?* A nanny who simply arrived at work on time and advised the parents whenever the child's supply of milk was running low shouldn't be taken for granted. Better yet is one whom the parents came to rely on for tasks like arranging play dates and doing grocery shopping.

- *Did any conflicts come up over disciplinary matters?* This is a common trouble area for parents and nannies, sometimes becoming the last straw before a nanny gets fired. For example, Shelley in Virginia, says "My oldest son is very strong-willed, and we hired one nanny who at first impressed me with her no-nonsense assertiveness. But it turned out she knew no other role than to lock heads with my son. After increasing conflicts, my son called me one day and said, 'Mommy, she locked me out of the house, and when I came back in she'd taken all the phones and locked them in her room, then told me, 'I'm going to tie you up and give your brother something to hit you with.' I came home and fired her, of course, but I still wish I'd trusted my instincts more when we first hired her."

- *Can you give examples of situations where the nanny had to handle an emergency or use independent judgment?* Even a nanny who is otherwise trustworthy and obedient may not be good in a crisis, and you'll want to know that in advance. If she has demonstrated an ability to handle crisis well, regard that as a major point in her favor.

- *Did you ever make unannounced checks of the nanny's performance?* If, for example, the parents showed up at home at odd times, or had friends who reported on how the nanny treated the kids at the playground, that's valuable verification of how she handles the kids when she thinks her employer isn't watching.

- *What's your warmest memory of the nanny?* This will help you get a picture of her as a person. The best nannies will bring special skills or interests to the relationship. For example, Amy, in Seattle, says, "Our nanny was endlessly creative and led the kids in playing charades, dress-up, and much more. They learned to make their own fun around the house, a side effect we hadn't expected."

- *What was the lowest point in your working relationship?* Don't skip this question: It may reveal something you'd have never thought to ask about, for example if the nanny protested mightily when the family wanted to get a dog or sulked after she didn't get a pay raise.

- *Is there anything else you think I'd like to know about?* Be alert to the reference's tone of voice here, and any hesitations. If information is still being held back, you may get a sense of that with this question.

At the end of the call, you'll probably have a strong sense of thumbs up or thumbs down. Still, in most cases it's worth calling the other references, for either confirmation or another view on the nanny's history.

Asking Nannies to Fill Out a Job Application

You don't have to pass out job applications, but some parents find it's a convenient way to collect and compare facts on nanny applicants. You can create a simple one based on our sample below. Then either email it to prospective nannies before you meet them, or ask them to fill one out at the beginning of your interview, while you do something else.

Sample Job Application Form

Application for Employment

Employer [*your own name and address*]

Name _____

Address _____

Telephone _____

Cell phone_____

Email _____

How did you hear about this job?_____

_____

Educational background

Highest level of education achieved _____

Have you had any formal training in child care? Please describe. _____

_____

Have you had CPR or first aid training? Please state type of training and dates
completed. _____

_____

Previous employment

Please fill in your employers for the past five years, starting with the most recent:

Employer's name _____

Employer's address _____

Employer's telephone _____

Nature of job _____

If child care, please state ages of children_____

_____

Dates worked _____

Reason for leaving _____

_____

Employer's name _____

Employer's address _____

Employer's telephone _____

Nature of job _____

Sample Job Application Form

Application for Employment, (cont'd)

If child care, please state ages of children_____

_____

Dates worked _____

Reason for leaving _____

Employer's name _____

Employer's address _____

Employer's telephone _____

Nature of job _____

If child care, please state ages of children_____

_____

Dates worked _____

Reason for leaving _____

Employer's name _____

Employer's address _____

Employer's telephone _____

Nature of job _____

If child care, please state ages of children_____

_____

Dates worked _____

Reason for leaving _____

Driving

Do you have a driver's license? _____

Do you have a car that can be used for our children? _____

If so, is your car insured? _____ Please provide us a copy of your proof of insurance.

Health

Do you smoke? _____

Do you have any physical limitations that would affect your ability to do this job?

Please describe. _____

Do you have any allergies to pets, scents, or food? Please describe. _____

_____

Sample Job Application Form

Application for Employment, (cont'd)

Are you available during the following hours? [*State the hours during which you want child care.*] _____

_____

Are you willing to make a minimum one-year commitment? _____

_____

Signed _____

Date _____

Getting to Know You: The Interview Process

You've probably eliminated a few nannies from consideration already. So it's time to pull out your short list and arrange initial interviews. We'll recommend following that up with a second interview for the final decision before hiring a nanny.

The First Interview

Plan to set aside at least an hour for each interview. Holding it in your own home is a good idea, so that the nanny can see where she'll be working, and you can introduce her to your children.

The children should not, however, be present for the entire interview (with the exception of a sleeping infant). It's distracting and also somewhat unfair to a nanny—the children may react badly to her on principle, realizing (if they're old enough) that their parents are about to leave them alone with a virtual stranger. Or they may love the nanny, leading you to decide too quickly that she's the right one. Children's intuition is valuable, but it's no substitute for independent investigation. For example, the children might correctly intuit that a particular nanny will be fun to play with, naturally overlooking the fact that she's irresponsible and a maniac behind the wheel.

If you're married or partnered, it's preferable, but not necessary for both of you to be at the interview. Your other half should obviously be available for the second interview, however. It's common for moms to be the primary one interacting with the nanny, but both of you should feel comfortable with and around her.

Scheduling more than one interview per day will probably wear you out. On the other hand, once you've started, you don't want to leave too much time between interviews. The hottest prospects may otherwise be snapped up by other parents while you're still deep in the interview process.

Keep the setting reasonably casual. You might, for example, offer tea or water. But in your hand should be a clipboard with a list of your questions, and notes from conversations with the prospective nanny's references, for comparison or follow-up purposes. You don't have to adhere slavishly to your list of questions—this is, in part, a friendly getting-to-know you conversation—but give yourself some time at the end to review your list and make sure you didn't forget anything.

USA TODAY Snapshots®

Résumés and reality

Is it common for a job applicant who has a promising résumé to not live up to your expectations when you interview him or her?

Yes **72%**

No **24%**

Don't know **4%**

Source: Robert Half International survey of 150 senior executives

By Jae Yang and Alejandro Gonzalez, USA TODAY 2009

If you've given the nanny an employment application, go over it and ask any questions it raises. For example, if there are gaps in her employment history, find out why.

Here's a list of questions to ask (a few of which you can skip if you asked the nanny to fill out an application form and the information is clearly covered there—but often it's worth hearing it straight from her, as well):

- *Why do you want to work as a nanny?* Good answers might include, "I love children," or "It's something I found I was good at after basically raising my little brothers." What you don't want to hear is that the nanny needs to earn some quick cash before starting grad school or her "real" career. You may also hear some answers like, "I've been laid off and unable to find a job in my area of expertise—I'm good with children so I thought I'd try this." You'll have to keep probing to find out whether she's acting out of desperation or genuine interest.

- *What sort of formal training have you had?* Find out your prospective nanny's highest level of educational achievement, plus any special classes or programs she's taken (including CPR and first aid). But don't automatically turn away someone whose education doesn't go past high school. As Vivian, in New Jersey says, "Let's face it, if these applicants had a lot on the ball, they probably wouldn't be looking for work as nannies. In fact, I've found that some of the brighter nannies I've hired had plans for the future that they didn't share with me—and within a year, they moved on."

- *Have you worked as a nanny before?* If yes, either get, or make sure the application she filled out already contains, a detailed list of when, for whom, and what her responsibilities were. If the answer is "No," ask about other relevant experience, such as caring for her own children or siblings, babysitting, camp counseling, volunteering, or teaching.

- *Are you legally able to work in the United States?* We advised asking this in the prescreening interview, but it's worth asking again and reminding her that you will need to check documents on the first day of work. If she's not legal and you want to hire someone who is, there's no point in continuing the interview.

- *What did you like most and least about each of your past nanny jobs?* Long answers are what you're looking for here, to get a sense of the nanny's interests and child-rearing philosophy. If, for example, she merely says, "The children were nice," you should follow up by asking, "What was nice about them?" and "What kind of activities did you do together?" Or if she says, "The children were out of control," ask, "What methods of control weren't working on them?"

- *Have you had any other relevant experience working with children?* The nanny may bring up her family and living situation, which are handy to know about. You'll learn not only about her experience, but you'll understand what responsibilities she'll be juggling while working for you. Also, if she'll be living in, ask whether she has a spouse, partner, or boyfriend, and how they're going to deal with the separation (making clear that you expect that person not to be staying at your house).

USA TODAY Snapshots®

Job candidate mistakes
In which job-application areas do candidates make the most mistakes?

Interview 32%
Résumé 21%
Cover letter 9%
Reference checks 9%
Interview follow-up 7%
Screening call 6%
Other 2%
Don't know 14%

Source: Robert Half Finance & Accounting survey of 1,414 CFOs of U.S. companies with 20 or more employees. Margin of error ±2 percentage points.

By Jae Yang and Sam Ward, USA TODAY 2006

- *How would you plan to spend a typical day with my child?* Of course, any applicant will be smart enough not to say, "Watching TV." Nevertheless, her answers will help indicate knowledge of the rhythm of a child's day and bring forth any special interests, such as art or outdoor activities.

- *What do you like to do in your spare time?* Perhaps the nanny will have interests that can further enrich your child's life. Or perhaps some incompatibilities will arise—you don't, for example, want an avid trumpet player or late-night partier if the nanny will be a live-in.

- *Tell me about your best friend.* This can get right to the heart of a person's values—or reveal an intense loneliness that should make you worry. You can also ask to call the friend as an additional reference.

- *Are you comfortable driving children around, and have you had any car accidents?* We'll show you below how to confirm the accident record with official sources, too. Also notice how the nanny arrived at your house. As Jack, a parent in Berkeley, California, noted, "One nanny we interviewed was driven to our house by her boyfriend, who waited for her in the car. That didn't seem to me like a positive sign of her independence, and we didn't hire her."

- *Do you smoke?* Smoking isn't a merely private matter. A smoker who agrees to refrain while on the job will, in all likelihood, be undergoing withdrawal pangs while caring for your kids—which can either put her in a bad mood or drive her out for a cigarette break.

- *What's your opinion of using drugs and alcohol?* Asking outright, "Do you use" is likely to get you a "no" answer. But many people will respond to a request that they express their opinions. Whether their stated positions match their personal practices is another matter, admittedly.

- *Do you have any health problems that affect your ability to work?* You can't just ask "How's your health," which will probably violate privacy laws, and could lead to a discrimination claim if you refuse to hire a person on a health basis that's unrelated to the job. However, you can make clear that the job involves some physical work, for example, carrying your child, loading a stroller into the car, and so on, and ask whether the applicant is up to that. If you observe that the nanny is in poor physical shape, or holds her back stiffly when getting out of a chair, you might want to make your own determination about whether she can handle the job. Some parents also ask a nanny to go to a doctor for a physical exam. This is permissible, as long as you don't expect to receive any results that have nothing to do with her ability to perform the job requirements. For example, you won't find out whether she is HIV+ or is taking birth control pills. You'll need to give her a job description to take to the doctor and a letter explaining that you would like a report on her fitness to do this job.

- *How would you handle a temper tantrum or discipline issue?*
  Jennifer of San Mateo County, California, notes, "Different
  forms of discipline are appropriate at different ages. When first
  interviewing nannies, I asked specifically, 'What's your discipline
  technique for a ten-month old?' Fortunately, all of the nannies
  I interviewed had the appropriate answer, which was distraction
  and redirection."

- *Have you handled any emergencies with children you've cared for?*
  Find out what happened, and how she reacted.

- *Have you ever spanked or used physical force or discipline on a child?*
  This question might feel nosy, but you have a right to ask. A good
  answer will make you feel
  more comfortable about
  the person you're hiring.
  A nervous or evasive
  answer will clue you
  into potential trouble,
  or at least make the job
  applicant aware that she's
  dealing with someone
  who's not going to make
  it easy for her to slide into
  a job and mistreat the
  kids once she gets there.

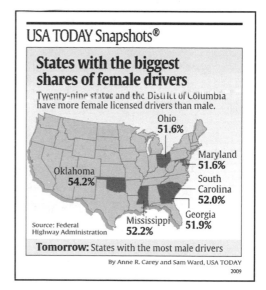

USA TODAY Snapshots®

**States with the biggest
shares of female drivers**

Twenty-nine states and the District of Columbia
have more female licensed drivers than male.

Ohio
51.6%

Maryland
51.6%

Oklahoma
54.2%

South
Carolina
52.0%

Georgia
51.9%

Mississippi
52.2%

Source: Federal
Highway Administration

Tomorrow: States with the most male drivers

By Anne R. Carey and Sam Ward, USA TODAY
2009

- *How would you respond if
  my child became upset or
  missed Mom or Dad?* Every nanny will face such issues and needs
  to be ready with various methods of both comforting the child
  and teaching him or her to deal with tough times.

- *Have you ever suspected that a child in your care was being sexually
  molested by someone?* Credit for this question goes to Gavin
  De Becker, author of *Protecting the Gift: Keeping Children and
  Teenagers Safe (And Parents Sane)*. De Becker is an expert on
  predicting and avoiding violent behavior. His excellent book—

while it delves into topics that some parents don't want to think about—is actually quite empowering, teaching parents how to trust and utilize their own intuition and recognize signs of actual danger. One of the worst things parents can do, De Becker notes, is to live in a state of denial. So the question above not only helps you understand the nanny's approach to child care, but makes sure that she herself is not a denier, who says something like, "That would never happen in a nice neighborhood like this!"

- *Would you be open to occasional schedule changes or extra hours?* If the nanny has family or other obligations, such flexibility might be impossible for her, so you'll need to take that into account.

- *What are you looking for in a nanny position?* This will help you understand whether she'll be happy working at your house. You can probably reassure her on some points. But if other aspects of what she wants simply won't match her workday reality, make that clear, and consider whether you think she's likely to stay around for the long term.

- *Do you know of any factors that might prevent you from working for us for at least a year?* Notice that you're not asking the applicant for an outright promise to stay for a year—that's impractical for anyone and doesn't really square with the at-will employment relationship that we recommend and describe in Chapter 9 (in which you can terminate the nanny at any time, but she can also leave at any time).

- *Do you have any questions for me?* She probably will—or she should.

- *Will you consent to us having a background check done on you?* As we'll explain later in this chapter, you can't perform such checks secretly. You'll need the prospective nanny to not only consent, but to sign a form proving her consent and providing her Social Security number, past addresses, and other information. Of course, there's no need to bother with this if you're sure you won't be hiring her—but if you think you might, leave a little time at the end of the interview for her to actually fill out the details on the form, or ask her to get it back to you as soon as possible.

If all has gone well so far, this is a good time to introduce the nanny to your children. For an infant, ask her to hold the baby, and watch how comfortable she looks. For older children, suggest that they show her their bedroom or a toy, to make them feel less awkward and give the nanny something to talk with them about. The more the nanny does to establish direct, personal communication with the kids—rather than looking to you for guidance or talking about them only in the third person—the better.

> **TIP**
> **Walk the applicant out to her car, and inquire about any signs of damage.** As Vivian, of Princeton, New Jersey, explains, "I learned this after one nanny lied to me about her accident record. The car looked fine parked in my driveway, but if I'd walked around it, I would have seen signs of the major accident she'd had. Her driving was indeed bad enough that I stopped letting the kids go in the car with her. Another benefit of looking at the applicant's car is that, if it's full of McDonald's bags or cigarette butts, that gives you clues as to her personal habits."

Finally, thank the prospective nanny for her time, and let her know when you will get in touch. If you feel pretty positive you'd like to hire her, also ask whether she's under any time restrictions.

Of course, we advise sleeping on your decision and doing a second interview and final background checks before saying, 'You're hired.' But if you've got serious cause to worry that she'll take another job, we understand. As a compromise, you could explain that your offer is subject to her passing the background checks, and then do them pronto. Another option is to start her off with a trial day or week, which we'll discuss below.

The Second Interview

Both you and the nanny were probably on your best behavior in the first interview. The question is, can you both sustain this and continue to feel comfortable with one another? A second interview will help establish this.

Of course, you don't want to simply reprise the first interview. Try changing the format a bit; for example, meet at the park with the kids, or have her meet only with the spouse or partner who couldn't attend the first interview. If you can afford it, an even better way to handle this is to invite her to care for the kids on a short, trial basis, as discussed next.

> **TIP**
> **At either the first or second interview, collect the nanny's proof of auto insurance.** Do so only if you'll be asking her to use her own car to drive your children, of course. A simple copy of her most recent certificate of coverage will do it.

Test Run: Hiring a Nanny for a Trial Period

Whether it's for a day, a few days, or for a week, hiring your prospective nanny for a short time will no doubt give you insight into her working style. It's not a perfect test, because you'll want to be either with her or close by the whole time. But it still leaves plenty of opportunity for a nanny who, for example, can't get herself out the door on time in the morning, or has no idea how to distract a cranky child, to show her true colors. And if you like what you see, it will make her first days of "official" work that much easier.

Show her around the house, as if it were her first day (as described in Chapter 10). And have her take on at least some of the responsibilities that she'll ultimately be handling, such as changing a diaper, making lunch for the kids, and even putting your child down for a nap (depending on your child's amenability to strangers). Try to stay out of your children's line of sight as much as possible during this time, so that you can watch the nanny, but the kids aren't distracted by you.

If there's time, also take the nanny and the kids to the park together, or to other places where you anticipate they'll spend a lot of time.

If possible, find a quiet bench and have them play or interact alone together.

Of course, during all this time, you'll have plenty of time to chat with the nanny and get to know her better personally. This is valuable for establishing rapport and giving you information that might help you if you do hire her. Even something as simple as knowing that she loves ballroom dancing will help you when it's time to choose a birthday present.

Is She for Real? Background Checks

Back to our Ronald Reagan refrain: Trust, but verify. A complete background check on a prospective nanny includes:

- verification of her identity and Social Security number
- verification of her educational and employment history
- a search for any available criminal or sex offense records, and
- a search of her driving records.

Most of these records are held in the deep dark computer hard drives of various government and court offices. Many courts and other agencies periodically upload some of these records to databases that are owned by companies that amass information on consumers' credit and histories; these are the databases that most criminal background check outfits either own outright or have a license to access. They are "proprietary"; that is, although they're made up of public information, they're not accessible by individuals like you. That's why, unless you personally visit every courthouse in every county where your prospective nanny lived, you'll have to make do with using one of these services.

Most of these services will deliver the whole works in one package. For example, many parents use ChoiceTrust (www.choicetrust.com), which as of this book's printing, charged $99 for its nanny check. Other options include www.4nannies.com and www.nannybackgrounds.com.

TIP

Can't afford a service? Ask the nanny to bring copies of her driving record, do your own check of the sex offender registry, and ask for any other independent verification of her qualifications that will help show that she is who she says she is, such as school transcripts or certificates. And don't forget the power of Google and other search engines! Put in the nanny's name in all possible permutations—she may allow members of the public to view her Facebook page and more, in which case you have good reason to check out what she tells others about her life.

While it's important not to skip this step, you should realize that a $99 background check is not failsafe. Not every county court or agency feeds up-to-date, accurate information to a nationally maintained database. And many convey only convictions that resulted in state prison time. Meanwhile, jail time for misdemeanors or convictions that were later reduced to a misdemeanor or "sealed" may not be revealed. On top of all this, the background checks often go back no more than ten years. The lesson is that a background check must be but one of several diligent efforts on your part to develop a true picture of the person who will be caring for your children.

CAUTION

Is your prospective nanny an undocumented immigrant? If so, your background check service might not get very far or may turn up information on someone else entirely. The services ordinarily use a nanny's Social Security number to run the check, and if she's undocumented, she either won't have a number, or may be using someone else's number.

In choosing a service, the key things to consider are:

- **It will do state- and county-specific criminal records searches.** Unfortunately, the only reasonably complete national database of criminal records is accessible to law enforcement only.

Background checkers must make do with a patchwork of reported information, gathered into private databases. So any agency that claims it will do an exhaustive, thorough national search is exaggerating. The more careful agencies take your nanny's list of past addresses and check personally with local law enforcement agencies there, which may mean sending an actual person to the courthouse to look at records. (Of course, the searcher won't find any crimes or convictions that occurred in a place where the nanny did not live.) Find out whether some actual "gumshoe" work will be done—the cheaper the cost of the check, the less likely that will happen.

- **It will search both felony and misdemeanor records.** You definitely want both. A misdemeanor may sound minor in theory, but depending on your state's laws, it can include offenses like petty theft, domestic violence, prostitution, drug possession, or DUI. Be aware, however, that not all misdemeanor convictions will show up, as explained earlier.

- **It charges extra for checking sex offender records.** If so, there may be no need to pay the extra. Thanks to Megan's Law, many states maintain sex offender registries that you can search on your own, online or by calling a hotline. Search online for "Megan's Law" and the name of your state, or see the list at the KlaasKids Foundation website, www.klaaskids.org.

- **The driving-records check includes every state the nanny has lived in.** Some services just check the state where you live. Be warned, however, that if your nanny has lived (or you now live) in Alaska, Washington, DC, New Hampshire, Oregon, or Pennsylvania, you'll have to ask your nanny to obtain a copy of her driving record on her own (through the local Department of Motor Vehicles). The nanny-check services won't be able to get a copy.

If you've gotten that far and all is well with your first-choice nanny, it's time to make an offer, as discussed in Chapter 9. If you're still choosing between candidates—all of whom you like—count your blessings, but don't spend too long deciding. Otherwise, another family may make the decision for you! Go with whichever one you like the best. Or quickly invite a friend to meet the candidates and weigh in.

What if the truths revealed in your background checks have disqualified all your candidates? If you've still got time, you could start your search again and perhaps refine your interview questions and techniques in light of what you've learned. Or, if the salary you're paying just doesn't seem to be bringing in nannies of adequate quality, you might want to rethink your options, based on the discussion in Chapter 1. Perhaps hiring a part-time nanny at a higher price, and working out an alternate arrangement on other days will be better.

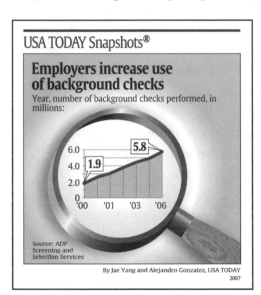

USA TODAY Snapshots®

Employers increase use of background checks

Year, number of background checks performed, in millions:

6.0
5.8
4.0
1.9
2.0
0
'00   '01   '03   '06

Source: ADP Screening and Selection Services

By Jae Yang and Alejandro Gonzalez, USA TODAY
2007

A final issue to consider, however, is whether you've set the bar too high. Yes, we urge checking out nannies' qualifications and basic record thoroughly—but some parents start out hoping for a nanny that doesn't really exist, perhaps one who will turn their babies into little artists or geniuses. As Susan, in Washington, DC, explains, "I realized at some point that the most important thing about the various women I'd hired—imperfect though they were—was that they kept my daughter safe. They were 'good-enough nannies.' You might have heard of the famous English psychologist Donald Woods Winnicott, who talks about the 'good-enough mother.' You can drive yourself insane trying to be the perfect mother, but sometimes you have to settle for good enough, and that's true with nannies, too."

Should You Disqualify a Nanny Who's Too Good-Looking?

In whispered conversations, many women ask friends whether it's okay for them to refuse to hire a nanny who's just so physically attractive that they're afraid their own husbands won't be able to resist the nearby temptation. (Similar issues could certainly come up with a manny, or a same-sex partner, but one doesn't hear about these as often.)

Certainly there's no legal rule on the matter. Being attractive isn't a protected category in any state, so no one can charge discrimination if you deny the youngest, cutest applicant the job.

It may come down to how much you will worry. Some women have no trouble feeling they can trust their husbands—or figure they can't keep every attractive woman out of his line of sight anyway. Others feel less certain or worry that an attractive nanny who's conveniently settled in the home environment—especially a live-in—is like putting chocolate in front of a chocaholic. Or some wives simply feel that they're going to feel frumpy next to the younger, attractive nanny.

And now for an uncomfortable dose of reality from employment attorney Bob King:

Lawsuits by nannies complaining of sexual harassment aren't uncom-mon. The quintessential case is a husband harassing a younger female nanny. He doesn't usually grope her or initiate physical contact, but instead may flirtatiously ask something like, "So, what would you do if I said, 'Gosh, I'd love to sleep with you?'" At that point the nanny may say, "I'd tell you, you're married and get away from me." Then the husband tries to laugh it off and says, "Right answer." But if such remarks become severe and pervasive they can constitute a hostile work environment, potentially giving the nanny grounds for a sexual harassment suit.

In any case, don't beat yourself up for feeling wary of the attractive job applicants; you're not the first. Face the issue honestly, and go with what makes you comfortable.

The Au Pair Option

Somewhere around the world right now, a young girl is looking at a brochure for an au pair program and thinking, "Hey, I could see America, learn some English, and get paid to do it!" If you're lucky, she's also thinking, "And I love taking care of children," as opposed to, "Hopefully, I won't be stuck with those runny-nosed creatures for too many hours a day."

The person might also be a young man, though that's fairly rare. The au pair program is open to both men and women, ages 18 to 26, with at least secondary school degrees, from around the world. Driven by the worldwide recession, the pool of young people signing up, particularly from Western Europe, is getting bigger than it's been in years.

In this chapter, we'll clue you in to how the au pair program works and, if you decide to hire an au pair, how to make the program work for you. You'll also hear a lot from an experienced au pair named Shylah—one whose host family couldn't speak highly enough about her—who went on to become a professional nanny in New Zealand. She gives an honest perspective on what a young person hopes for and experiences in this unusual role.

USA TODAY Snapshots®

Young Americans staying home
Percentage of Americans ages 18 to 24 who have traveled outside the USA in the past three years (by number of trips):

None **70%**
Three or more **9%**
Two **7%**
One **14%**

Source: National Geographic, 2006 Geographic Literacy Study

By David Stuckey and Suzy Parker, USA TODAY 2006

> 💡 **TIP**
>
> **Get ready for a new personal relationship.** According to a program consultant we spoke to at one au pair agency, "Having someone living in your home takes some getting used to, but it often creates a relationship for life. We have one host mother who, after her kids had grown up, took a trip in which she visited all her previous au pairs!"

Happy With the Male Au Pair

Todd Doing says his home in Chappaqua, New York, is no place for discrimination when choosing the right person to watch over his two boys. He and his wife, Susan, have done something still rare in American child care: They've picked a man.

A 6-foot-4 German basketball player, no less, who does the boys' laundry, makes their lunches, helps with their dinner, and kisses them good night.

In his accented English, Fabian Spitzer, 23, remembers friends back in Chemnitz razzing him about assuming duties as a nanny in America. But no matter, he says, "I love to see smiling kids. I love to have fun."

"I've always been a person who judges people by who they are, as far as what they do," says Todd Doing, a building contractor, "rather than what they look like or what their sex is."

Some observers say that kind of tolerance, while still the exception, could trigger a wider acceptance of young men as caregivers for children in the home. The Intelligence Factory, a trend-spotting unit of advertising agency Young & Rubicam, predicts that "as more older men become fathers, a new breed of young, athletic male nannies will emerge to take on the more physically demanding aspects of the job.... teaching a child to ride a bike, playing ball in the park."

Doing couldn't agree more. He characterizes himself as a "bit out of shape." At the end of a long workday, his enthusiasm for a little rough-and-tumble playtime with sons Jim, 8, and Eric, 5, is maybe not all it could be. "It's like 'Daddy's home. Let's play,'" he says dryly. Thankfully, Spitzer now burns up the boys' afternoon energy with basketball, soccer, bike riding, swimming, and occasional calisthenics.

"He's got my 8-year-old doing push-ups and sit-ups with him," Doing says. "He definitely is teaching them physical things, which is good, because I just don't have the time for it."

 "'Manny' Poppins," by Gregg Zoroya, September 19, 2000.

Who Gets What in This Cultural Exchange

The basic idea of the au pair program is that, in return for receiving up to 45 hours a week of child care, you pay a modest wage—more like a stipend, really—and help the au pair learn English and have an American cultural experience. As Brenda, in Buffalo, New York, sums up, "An au pair is kind of an employee, kind of a family member, kind of an exchange student, kind of a big sister, and kind of a babysitter. It's a conglomeration of roles, with the result that it's great if it works out—but it doesn't always work out."

USA TODAY Snapshots®

What adults say is their idea of the American Dream

Free to accomplish anything	74%
Free to say/do what they want	68%
Children financially better off	64%
Being financially secure	61%

Note: Percentage rating these 8-10 on a 10-point scale, in which 10 is the perfect definition
Source: Pew Charitable Trusts survey of 2,119 adults Jan. 27-Feb. 8

By Anne R. Carey and Sam Ward, USA TODAY 2009

Although the concept is fairly simple, the au pair program is highly structured, being governed by U.S. immigration laws and administered through various private agencies as well as the U.S. State Department (DOS). An au pair receives a special cultural exchange visa called a J-1. Like every visa, it has rules and time limits and can be taken away if these aren't met.

Fortunately, you don't have to get tied up with the visa, background checks, or associated administrative hassles—the intermediary agency will take care of all this for you (for a price). But you should understand what you can expect from the agency that helps you find an au pair and what basic responsibilities you'll be taking on.

Your Responsibilities When Hosting an Au Pair

The government has also set forth rules on what you need to be and do for your au pair. First, in terms of basic eligibility, you and your spouse or partner must:

- live within an hour's driving distance of an au pair program coordinator's home (someone authorized to act on the sponsoring agency's behalf in both routine and emergency matters relating to the au pair and who will visit or contact you regularly, especially in the first two months, to see how things are going)

- be interviewed by an agency representative

- pass a background investigation in which you'll provide employment and personal character references (as well as for any adults living full time in your household)

- be able to afford all your hosting obligations

- be U.S. citizens or legal permanent residents

- be fluent in English

- not plan on the au pair supervising any children under the age of three months (and if you'll have children this young, show that an adult will be there to care for them)

- not plan on the au pair caring for any special-needs child, unless the au pair has specifically relevant prior experience, skill, or training

- have space in your house to provide the au pair with a private bedroom, and

- cooperate with the sponsoring agency's preparation of detailed materials to give the au pair, including a profile of your family and community and of the educational institutions where she'll be able to take classes.

In addition, once the au pair arrives, you'll be responsible for the following:

- **Initial supervision.** For the first three days of the au pair's stay, a member of your family or a contact person must be present in the house.

- **Pay.** You'll pay a preset amount—as of this book's printing, $139 per week. Diana, from Marin County, California, says, "We hired an au pair from Sweden when my son was one and a half and my daughter was four. We did the math, and there was really no more cost-effective way to have child care. It meant that I could go for an early-morning run, and work in San Francisco without worrying about getting home late."

- **Limited work days and hours.** This isn't a ticket to round-the-clock help. The au pair can work only 45 hours per week and no more than ten hours per day or five and one-half days per week. (An easier way to remember that last part is that she must have at least one and a half days off per week.) You don't have to work out an unchanging schedule—flexibility is one of the great things about having an au pair—but for clarity's sake, you should set out general work hours. So, for example, you could ask her to work from 9 a.m. to 5 p.m. weekdays and from 10 a.m. to 3 p.m Saturday, or from 8 a.m. to 5 p.m. weekdays with weekends off; or any other variation. Time of day is not an issue from the State Department's standpoint; if you'd like her to babysit in the evenings, that's okay.

 TIP
Tell a prospective au pair your desired schedule in advance. If, for example, you'd like your au pair to work weekends but she plans to use that time to explore the United States or stay with friends, you're probably better off finding someone else. Stacey Frank, of Agent Au Pair in San Francisco, explains, "Most au pairs are willing to work weekends, but she should know that ahead of time. A lot of our host families will run their proposed schedule by us first—sometimes we'll say, 'Yes, it's within the regulations, but no au pair is likely to agree to this.' For example, one set of parents wanted an au pair to work until 8 p.m. Friday night, then start at 6 a.m. Saturday morning and work until 9 a.m.; then work again from Saturday 3 p.m. until 8 p.m.; then get up at 6 a.m. Sunday morning and work until 9 a.m. That would have meant the au pair couldn't go out Friday or Saturday nights and would have always had to get up early on weekends. We eventually found an au pair willing to follow this schedule every other weekend."

- **Inclusion in family activities.** You're expected to share meals, outings, holiday parties, and other family activities with your au pair. If you and your family go camping, skiing, to Disneyland, or on any other vacation travel, you must take the au pair with you (and pay her way).

> (!) CAUTION
>
> **What about housework?** An au pair is not a housekeeper, so you're not supposed to hand her any major cleaning tasks. However, she should be treated like a member of your family, so you can ask her to pitch in on light housework like washing dishes, cleaning up after the kids, feeding the pets, and cooking (if she knows how).

- **Weekends off.** Once a month, your au pair must be allowed a complete weekend to herself. Consider this essential for her mental health. In the words of Shylah, former au pair from New Zealand, "The time spent with friends on weekends was the happiest in the USA. We went shopping, to the movies, and to parties. It was essential to spend time away from the families and to vent and unwind. I was, after all, very young then. Now, as a nanny, my happiest memories are usually things the children have said or done."

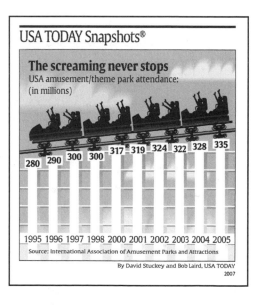

USA TODAY Snapshots®

The screaming never stops
USA amusement/theme park attendance:
(in millions)

280 290 300 300 317 319 324 322 328 335

1995 1996 1997 1998 2000 2001 2002 2003 2004 2005

Source: International Association of Amusement Parks and Attractions

By David Stuckey and Bob Laird, USA TODAY
2007

What Happens If You Make Your Au Pair Do Extra Hours

Playing fast and loose with the hours limits is not a good idea. For one thing, it may get you into trouble with your local coordinator, to whom the au pairs are told to report such issues. Shylah also relates her unhappiest memory of time spent as an au pair: "My work week always ended when Friday dinner was finished and I'd cleared the dishes away. If the parents wanted me to babysit after that, it was arranged well in advance, because I went out every weekend. (I'd learned to pack a bag and leave on Friday night, after several Saturday mornings were spent with me getting up and heading upstairs only to discover that the parents had gone out and left all the children at home!)

"Anyway, one Friday I was clearing the dishes away, ready to go out. The father came up and said 'By the way, we have plans tonight.' I replied, 'So do I.' He didn't say anything, but went away and got the mother. They asked me to come into the living room. The mother then sent the children outside, closed the door, and proceeded to tell me how ungrateful I was. She said I needed to consider how lucky I was to have use of the car and Internet (both of which were standard things for au pairs), and before I complained to my coordinator about working an hour or two more than I was supposed to (I usually worked ten hours overtime each week), I needed to realize that things could get a lot worse. I was then told that I was having my car taken away and the next step was to be the Internet. I was annoyed at being treated like a child. They were actually trying to ground me!"

- **Vacation.** You must give your au pair two paid weeks of vacation time per year. (That means you pay the usual $139—but you don't need to pay the vacation expenses.)
- **Arrange and pay for classes.** The U.S. government expects you to not only give the au pair opportunities to learn about life in the United States, but to pay up to $500 per year for some actual

education—at least six semester hours of college-level coursework. And you must help her sign up. Many au pairs sign up for English classes, especially if their required English proficiency turns out to have been overstated.

- **Attend a conference.** The au pair organization will sponsor regular family day conferences, and you'll need to attend at least one during the placement year.

There are limits to your responsibilities, however. For one thing, unlike with your own children, you don't have to pay every last expense the au pair incurs. Telephone calls, for example, are not your responsibility. Nor are gas and entertainment when she's out on her own, for example, taking weekend trips or spending the evening with friends.

> **TIP**
>
> **Got school-age children?** Look into the EduCare Program, which is a specialized part of the au pair program that lines up au pairs for families with children who require care before and after school hours. (Note: If you also have preschool children, you can't use this program unless you prove that you've made alternative, full-time arrangements for their supervision.) The EduCare au pair may work no more than ten hours per day and a maximum of 30 hours per week. You'll pay 75% of the weekly rate paid to a regular au pair. And you'll need to help her sign up for at least 12 hours of academic credit or its equivalent during the program year and pay up to the first $1,000 of the costs.

What You Can Expect From the Sponsoring Agency

What a relief it can be to turn the initial legwork in finding child care over to someone else! A qualified au pair sponsoring agency—and you'll want to make sure to hire one that's received authorization from the U.S. State Department, as we'll discuss below—will screen every prospective au pair who gets included on its list. The agency will:

- hold a personal interview with the applicant (and prepare a written report about it, which you're entitled to see)
- administer a psychometric exam and create a personality profile of the applicant
- check the applicant's school, job, and personal references
- check that she has an international driver's license
- require her to undergo a physical exam, and
- conduct a criminal background check.

In the course of this, the agency is expected to make sure that each applicant:

- has experience in child care
- is physically up to the tasks ahead
- has basic skills in English, and
- in the case of some agencies, is a nonsmoker.

If an applicant makes it through this screening and signs up for placement, the agency will also give her some training in child safety and development. This must include at least eight hours of child safety instruction (of which at least four relate to infants) and at least 24 hours of child development instruction (of which at least four relate to children under the age of two).

The agency will also help the au pair prepare for her U.S. stay. It will arrange health, accident, and auto insurance, offer language courses, and remain an ongoing resource in case difficulties arise. It will even pay the au pair's plane fare and other transportation to your house (using the fees paid by you and other parents).

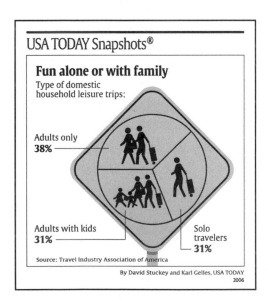

USA TODAY Snapshots®

Fun alone or with family
Type of domestic household leisure trips:

Adults only
38%

Adults with kids
31%

Solo travelers
31%

Source: Travel Industry Association of America

By David Stuckey and Karl Gelles, USA TODAY 2006

How the Timing Works

You can start your au pair search at any time—it's not a seasonal thing, though the agencies may schedule arrival dates on a rotating basis, such as once every month or two. Don't wait until the last minute, however. It can take weeks or months to complete the paperwork and interview process and find an au pair you like.

An au pair can stay in the United States for up to twelve months, with a maximum of one twelve-month extension. However, most au pairs prefer to leave after one year or less.

Choosing Your Au Pair Agency

As you can see, the choice of an au pair agency is an important one. Although you must start with the State Department's list of designated sponsors, and there are only 12 agencies on that list, they're not all the same. Realize, too, that you'll be relying on this agency for some very important tasks, including adequately screening the au pairs, finding a good match for you, training the au pair, and providing ongoing support for you and her.

> **RESOURCE**
> **For the State Department's list of designated au pair agencies:** Go to http://exchanges.state.gov; under Quick Links, click "Au Pair Program;" then over to the right, click "Current Sponsors List;" and select "Au Pair" from the drop-down menu. Note that most of the agencies are in California, so it's unlikely there will be one near you. That's okay, so long as they have local coordinators in your area.

Beware of Au Pair Scams

If you believe what you see on the Internet, there are a lot more ways to find an au pair than through the 12 designated agencies.

At the most benign end of the spectrum, some websites let au pairs post their photos and personal profiles, and then when you've chosen one, direct you to one of the designated agencies to complete the process. These websites aren't necessarily doing anything wrong, although some parents feel misled when they discover that the fee that they may pay to the sites covers only a small portion of what's involved in getting the au pair here.

More disturbing are agencies that line you up with people who are already in the United States, usually on a tourist or student visa. With few exceptions, the terms of their visas do not allow them to take paid work. Because enforcement of the no-work rule for visitors and students is fairly lax, you may get away with hiring these people. But understand that without a legitimate agency in the picture, you won't enjoy the same kind of official support that you will with a legal au pair. You may even find that your au pair has to leave the country on short notice.

At the far end of the spectrum are outright scam operations, where you're more likely to have your money or identity stolen than to receive child care of any sort. For example, reports have surfaced of families who thought they were communicating with a prospective au pair, and at her request, sent money for airfare or to move the process along. As you might expect, that's the last they heard from her.

Although such scams are said to originate primarily in Nigeria, Ghana, Cameroon, or another developing country, the emails may pretend to be from any country in the world. And they're getting more sophisticated than you might expect, involving multiple players such as travel agents, university professors, and people posing as parents and references.

The bottom line: Start with one of the designated agencies, and tell them immediately if you receive any request for money directly from someone claiming to be a prospective au pair.

Below are some things to research or ask about when choosing among agencies. Some of the information you'll be able to find on their websites; some you'll need to ask in a phone call; and some you may not be able to get answers on at all—but it's worth a try.

- *How long will the process take?* Make sure their scheduling fits yours. A good agency can start hooking you up with potential matches within a day or two. But you'll also need to make sure that their schedule of au pair group arrival dates (they're usually brought to the United States in bunches) works for you. For example, if they bring a group in once a month, and you'll be out of town for the relevant day of that month, you may have to wait another month.

- *How much will I need to pay in total?* Find out how the fee structure works, both at the initial application phase and after your au pair arrives, for example if you're not happy with her or you lose your job and can no longer afford to pay her. If one agency's fees look significantly lower than the others', don't assume it's a bargain—they may later ask you to foot the bill for other costs that would simply be included in other agencies' basic fees.

- *Is your pay structure for local coordinators based in part on bonuses, and if so, for what?* It's good to know what incentives your local coordinators are operating under. For example, some receive a bonus for every au pair who successfully stays with her host family. Although meant as positive reinforcement, this should also make you a bit nervous: Your coordinator will have every interest in convincing you to keep your au pair, even if she's just not a good match for your family.

- *What's your ratio of host families to local coordinators?* The more families your coordinator has to take care of, the less individual attention you're likely to get. For example, Helene Young of USAuPair in Lake Oswego, Oregon, says, "We don't assign our reps more than 15 families, and most are comfortable with about ten. That way the reps can bond with the au pairs, and get to know the families really well. If something starts bubbling, the reps can jump in there right away. Sometimes one of our reps is even the one to tell a family that we think something's not right and their au pair should go home. The safety of the children is, after all, paramount."

- *Can I talk directly to the local coordinator?* You'll probably start the process with the agency's national headquarters. But once your au pair arrives, your primary contact will be a local person who is supposed to keep tabs on you and the au pair and help resolve any difficult situations. So, it would be nice to make sure you're comfortable with that person before submitting your application to that agency, if possible. (It won't always be possible.)

- *What's your procedure for matching families with potential au pairs?* Some agencies pride themselves on providing one-on-one matching. In other words, instead of hitting you with a slew of applications, they very carefully identify two to five candidates who closely meet your criteria, then present their information to you. The agency allows you to interview and choose among the selected candidates (or to say "No, please give us further options") without the pressure of other families having access to the same group. That saves you time and the bother of falling in love with a candidate only to discover that she's disqualified based on one of your core criteria, perhaps because she has no experience driving in snow. But some parents feel that this is too limiting and wish they knew more about the other au pairs on file. Conversely, some agencies simply make all of their candidates available to you, for example on a website with their photos and profiles. But this can lead to situations where you think, for example, "Veronique is the one for us!" only to have another family sign her up ten minutes before you.

- *If you suggest candidates who are being transferred from another U.S. family, will you let us talk to that family?* For obvious reasons, it's in your interest to find out why the match didn't work out. Unfortunately, some agencies say "Yes, you can contact them," but in practice, you won't learn anything. That's because these agencies have asked their families to sign nondisclosure agreements, which are promises that the families won't talk about a failed placement. According to the agreements, if a family breaks its promise and talks about the placement, it won't get its money refunded. So, ask whether the agency uses nondisclosure agreements with provisions like this.

- *What benefits do you offer your au pairs?* For example, if the agency buys them health insurance, that's one less thing you'll have to worry about.

USA TODAY Snapshots®

Learning the lingo

Number of children in China studying English: **200 million**

Number of children in the USA studying Chinese: **24,000**

Source: Department of Education
By David Stuckey and Sam Ward, USA TODAY 2006

- *What countries do most of your au pairs come from?* No one agency has the resources to represent au pairs from the whole world. Typically, they draw from 40 to 60 countries—which is particularly relevant if you're hoping for an au pair from a certain country (perhaps one who can cook the food of that country or teach your kids its language).

- *What type of psychometric exam do you give your au pairs?* You'd think that testing would be standardized—but it's not. An agency could take a fluffy personality test off the Internet that had nothing to do with child care and give it to the candidates, and still be meeting the regulations. And you won't be given the actual results, you'll just be told that your candidate "passed." Finding out which test was used will tell you less than learning what's on the exam. Evaluate its effectiveness using your common sense. Follow up by asking whether they ever fail anyone. If not, it's a red flag.

- *What happens if our au pair doesn't work out?* Ideally, the agency will either help resolve the problem or line you up with a new au pair on a discounted basis. But don't expect a full refund. No agency can guarantee a person's personality, and by the time the au pair comes to you, the agency will have already laid out money for her screening, training, plane fare, insurance, and more.

- *How much child care experience do you require for au pairs caring for children* over *the age of two?* (If your children are under age two, you can skip this one.) As we mentioned above, State Department regulations require au pairs to have a minimum of 200 hours of infant experience before being placed with a family with kids under two. But there's no minimum requirement for kids over age two. That means that, in theory, you could end up with an au pair for your three-year-old whose child care references are actually based on 15 hours of babysitting. If you have older kids, you should look for an agency that has raised its standards above the State Department's, for example by demanding that all its au pair candidates have 200 hours of child care experience.

- *What's the ratio of your training class instructors to au pairs?* It may sound like we're getting nitpicky here, but the reassurance that you gain from knowing that your au pair will have been "trained" in child safety and development—or in some cases "CPR certified"—may be a false one. Realize, first of all, that these trainings usually take place in the United States after a group of au pairs has arrived from all over the world. (Some agencies do, however, conduct a preliminary orientation in the au pair's home country.) The training is in English—a language with which many of the students may be only minimally comfortable. If you discover that your au pair will be in a conference room with 150 other students and only one teacher, you should definitely worry that she won't be getting much individual attention; perhaps not enough to even see whether she has understood the basics.

> **TIP**
> **"Our agency deliberately doesn't do advance CPR certification."** So says Helene Young, of USAuPair, explaining that, "We include basic CPR training in our workshop, but we've found that most au pairs still need time to get comfortable in English before they absorb the details. We suggest to families, 'Wait around 60 days until the au pair's English language gets to where she understands, and then sign her up for a CPR certification course.'"

After you've selected an agency to work with, it will ask you to pay an application fee, to send photos of everyone in your household, to provide personal and employment references, and to fill out forms or write short descriptions of:

- your children's needs
- your preferred form of recreation
- your religious practices
- the likely schedule you'll ask your au pair to work, and
- how you'll provide transportation while the au pair is staying with you.

The agency does, after all, need to make sure that you're a suitable host family. And it's gathering information to give your prospective au pair, so that she can get a sense of who you are before saying "yes." She's struggling with the same limitations as you are. As Shylah explains, "It's very difficult to know a family before you meet them, because people can say pretty much whatever they want in an essay in order to make themselves seem an ideal match. I stayed with my original family for only a month before finding a new position, as we just did not match well."

Choosing an Au Pair

Because au pairs, by definition, come from another country, you won't get to meet prospective ones in person before making your choice. Even after the agency has gone over your application and preselected likely candidates for you, making final choices by reading paperwork and talking over the phone is no easy task.

As Brenda describes, "I spent a lot of time researching, reading the au pairs' applications looking for hidden messages, and interviewing. I took way too long to make the first offer, and she turned out to be a disaster! She had no idea how to interact with the kids. On paper she was fantastic; she had two brothers and was the oldest, so I thought that she must be used to taking family responsibility; she played basketball, so I assumed she'd be active and take the boys outside and play with them; she was an assistant teacher in a kindergarten, so I figured she must have been well trained from that; she loved to cook; and she spoke Spanish, a language I thought would be great to have in the home. But she lasted two weeks. I realized then that personality is the most important thing, and there was no way I could really gauge that from afar. I told my husband, 'I'm terrible at this, you pick the next one.' He picked someone I wouldn't have looked at twice, and she was fantastic. And he did it again for the next au pair, although the third one he picked was not so good."

You can see why some parents choose to fly to the au pair's country for an interview—or at least learn how to use Skype or a similar online video chat program. In any case, it's a good excuse for a vacation, and the stakes are high: The person you choose will be living in your house, sitting at your dinner table, and riding in your car on upcoming vacations.

You should be able to arrange with the au pair agency to meet more than one prospect during your trip. Some parents even take a trip before signing up with an au pair agency, meet a young girl that they like, and then contact an agency to arrange for her to come (referred to as a prematch). The agencies aren't crazy about such arrangements, however, because both the au pairs and the parents tend to regard the agency as a trivial intermediary in the process, which reduces their authority in resolving any disputes that later arise.

If you can't arrange a trip to meet au pair candidates in person, however, here are some steps for making the most of the materials and screening methods available to you:

1. **Carefully review the written materials.** The agency should provide you with a packet on each candidate (exactly what's in that packet depends on the agency). These materials won't tell you everything, but they're an important starting point and can help you develop questions for when you talk.

> **TIP**
> **Consider whether parts of the written materials leave room for fudging.** For example, if the application asks the au pair to check "yes" or "no" as to whether she can drive, anyone minimally capable of handling a car will probably check "yes." That's what happened with the au pair Diana, in Marin County, California, chose. Diana explains, "When she got here, she said, 'Well, I'm really not very good at driving, and I'm not comfortable with it.' I said, 'In that case I definitely don't want you driving my kids!'"

2. **Decide what type of personality you're looking for.** Remember, you not only want someone who will be good with your kids, but with whom you can comfortably live. As Brenda in Buffalo points out, "I've talked to different families who have au pairs, and some want very different things than I do. For example, do you want someone who's eager to join in all the fun all the time? Or one who gives you space? Some moms want a constant companion to talk with, but there's no way I'd want that!"

3. **Have more than one phone conversation.** There's good news here—many agencies will arrange for you to make these phone calls free of charge. During your first conversation, make clear that you won't be making a decision during that call. Start by telling the applicant about your family. Then ask about the basics—her experience, motivation, and so forth—even if they've been covered in her application. Ask about her friends and family and her likes and dislikes, to get a sense of what she's like as a person. Also look at the list of questions provided for interviewing regular nannies in Chapter 7. If you feel good about the

conversation, sleep on it, then develop follow-up questions for the next one. Keep talking until you're comfortable that you have a good sense of this person and have resolved any doubts or prickles of intuition. Make sure both you and your spouse or partner are involved in these conversations, even if not at the same time.

4. **Write up and send her your house rules.** For example, you might specify no overnight boyfriends, no having friends visit while you're working, and no partying all night. If this makes the au pair feel like her life is being overly restricted, it's better if you each make your decision accordingly.

5. **Talk with any previous host families.** Your best candidate may be someone who is already in the United States and switching from another host family. Some arrangements just don't work out, so don't automatically assume the problem was with the au pair. But if it was, you'll, of course, want to hear about it and hopefully have chosen an agency that will allow this. In other cases, the au pair might have been an au pair before, and maxed out her time in the United States, then waited for two years, after which she's allowed to come back again as an au pair.

TIP

If you get a great au pair, treat her right. This means, first of all, abiding by the basic wage, hour, and other rules and regulations, and showing up for any trainings or conferences. Don't try to make your agency complicit in sneaking around these rules—any agency that will turn a blind eye is perhaps not the one you want screening your au pairs in the first place. Also pay attention to the personal side: As Shylah says, "It's difficult to be so young and living away from your friends and family—on the other side of the world!" For further suggestions on how to make your child care provider want to stick around and live up to your expectations, see Chapter 11.

How Much Will the Au Pair Hang Around Your House?

Considering your au pair isn't likely to have friends in your area, you might worry that she'll need constant entertainment. For most parents, however, this is the least of their issues.

For example, Diana says, "Every day when I got home, the au pair would have her miniskirt and high heels on and be off to the Silver Peso to play pool. I think she wanted to find a way to stay in the United States. By the end of her stay, she had actually found an American man to marry, though she divorced him three years later. But I did feel comfortable that my kids were well cared for."

On the other hand, given the young age of some au pairs, you may sometimes feel a need to step in with advice. Vivian, in Princeton, says, "Even the best au pairs we've hired had some issues. Some were so gullible, they'd go out with any boy—or even a taxi driver—who looked at them for more than 1/100th of a second. Instead of my au pairs taking care of my kids, I ended up taking care of some of my au pairs."

Getting Your Employment Agreement and Other Instructions on Paper

When at last you've decided which nanny you'd like to hire, let her know as soon as possible, probably by phone. That way, she'll put an end to her job search. But you've got a couple of other tasks to take care of before she shows up for work, which we'll describe in this chapter. These include:

- drafting a contract that formally lays out the terms and conditions of the nanny's employment and describes the job

- drawing up a list of emergency contacts

- creating a form authorizing the nanny or au pair to handle medical matters on behalf of your child in case of an emergency, and

- creating a notebook containing other useful information about your house and children.

The more you put down in writing, the less you'll have to remember to tell your nanny in person. Of course, you'll still need to go over all these things with her to make sure she understands—and even more so if her English is not great. But no matter what, it's helpful to put everything in writing as a way of organizing your thoughts and giving both of you something to refer back to.

Drafting an Employment Agreement

Many parents' first response to the idea of creating an employment contract is, "Oh no, I'd never want to introduce so much formality into the relationship." But they usually change their minds after thinking through the purpose and advantages of creating an employment contract, namely to:

- summarize everything you've told your nanny about what the job involves, how much you'll pay her, the benefits, and more

- obtain the nanny's formal acceptance of those terms and conditions, and

- have on hand a written agreement covering key issues in case the nanny later claims the job entailed something different.

In other words, a contract between you and your nanny isn't a silly formality that makes lawyers happy—it's a useful tool for reaching a mutual understanding. As employment attorney Bob King (founder of Legally Nanny®, a highly regarded law firm providing legal and tax advice to household employers and domestic employment and homecare agencies in Irvine, California, explains), "It's rare to get any objections from the nannies, especially after parents point out that the contract benefits them, too. Both sides are agreeing to terms and making sure there's no misunderstanding. If the nanny won't sign the contract, that's a cautionary flag. If I were a parent, I'd ask 'Why not, what's problematic about the contract?' and discuss it right then."

We provide a sample contract, drafted for a fictional family, below. Modeling your own based on this one should be fairly simple; when in doubt, mention everything that you feel your nanny should know about or be entitled to (for example, if you'll be paying health benefits or providing her with a cell phone). At the same time, avoid making promises that you might later want to back out of, such as for an annual raise or bonus.

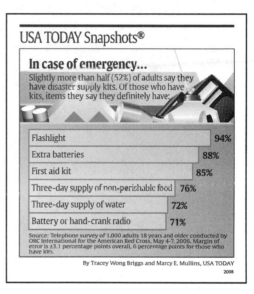

USA TODAY Snapshots®

In case of emergency...

Slightly more than half (52%) of adults say they have disaster supply kits. Of those who have kits, items they say they definitely have:

Flashlight	94%
Extra batteries	88%
First aid kit	85%
Three-day supply of non-perishable food	76%
Three-day supply of water	72%
Battery or hand-crank radio	71%

Source: Telephone survey of 1,000 adults 18 years and older conducted by ORC International for the American Red Cross, May 4-7, 2006. Margin of error is ±3.1 percentage points overall, 6 percentage points for those who have kits.

By Tracey Wong Briggs and Marcy E. Mullins, USA TODAY
2008

You'll notice that the sample contract includes mention of a 15-day probationary period. You could make this trial period longer or shorter, or not include it at all. The idea is to make it more comfortable to fire the nanny early on if things don't work out. (For tax purposes, if you fire her within a trial or probationary period and haven't yet paid her $1,700, you don't need to worry about withholding, as described in Chapter 5. You'd pay her the same way you would a babysitter. But if you do end up keeping her on, you'll need to retroactively calculate and withhold tax.)

Remember, though, that even without a probationary period, you're free to fire your nanny at any time—that is, without the customary two weeks' notice—and for any reason that's not illegal. This is what's called "employment at will," which is also spelled out in the sample contract. Unless you actually promise to maintain the employment relationship for a certain length of time or say you'll terminate a person only for good cause, the law presumes that you're an at-will employer. You're making that extra clear by including it in the contract. It's a handy provision to have if you lose trust in your nanny and don't want her in your house anymore. We're not saying, however, that nanny terminations should always be done on the spot, with no notice—see Chapter 12 for more on terminating a nanny.

Be aware that the employment-at-will doctrine applies to the nanny as well as to you; that is, she can quit at any time, with no notice. You might want to talk with her about this possibility ahead of time and request that, if possible, she let you know her plans a week or two in advance. That will help you line up alternate care (though you should be scouting around for this already, just in case). Reassure her that you won't simply fire her as soon as she gives notice, which some parents have been known to do.

> **CAUTION**
> **Do you live in Montana?** In that case, the laws on at-will employment are a little more complex. Montana protects employees who have completed an initial "probationary period" from being fired without cause.

The sample contract also contains an optional confidentiality clause, which reminds the nanny that you don't want your personal business discussed with others and gives you legal grounds to sue if she violates this. The confidentiality clause can be helpful to more than just celebrities, as it protects people's personal, business, and financial information. Bob King notes, "Celebrities often want the clause, but so do businesspeople, like investment advisers or CEOs. The reason is that they may have insider information that can be left out on coffee table or discussed over dinner. If the nanny saw or heard it and then spread it around, stocks or other investments could be materially affected." By the way, the confidentiality agreement loses its force if you do something illegal—the nanny is allowed to go to the authorities about that.

If you intend to ask the nanny to accompany you on vacations, cover this in the contract. Our sample includes the standard arrangement of paying regular hours plus a bonus for staying overnight, but your state's law might require something else. In California, for example, employment attorney Bob King explains, "The law requires you to pay your nanny for any time traveled beyond normal commuting time. So if, for example, she normally drives 15 minutes from her home to yours, you'd have to pay her for the 15 extra minutes it will take her to get to the airport, plus the hours she spends on the plane, and any other travel time until she reaches the final destination (such as a hotel). There are legal ways to establish a different travel time pay rate in advance, but that's the basic rule that your contract would need to accommodate."

> ### Celebs who've sued their nanny for violating a confidentiality agreement
>
> *Actor Rob Lowe and his wife Sheryl Berkoff, soccer star David Beckham and his wife Victoria (also known as Posh Spice), and Lisa Marie Presley have all done so. Tom Cruise is said to require such thorough confidentiality agreements— with violations dealt with swiftly and harshly—that no household employee would dream of violating them.*

If you're hiring a live-in nanny, you'll of course want to tailor the contract for that. Explain that you'll provide both room and board (you shouldn't expect her to pay for her own food, other than luxury items). Set forth any additional house rules that apply, even when the nanny is off the job (but still in your home), such as no overnight guests, no alcohol or drugs, no use of certain rooms in your house or office supplies, and if she has a mobile phone, no use of your telephone except for family-related calls. You might also want to specify house "quiet hours," during which you expect she won't turn on a TV or stereo.

Employment Agreement

This contract is made between Angela Roeper and Conrad Bradshaw ("Parents"), living at 133 Longview Vista, Keene, NH 03431, 603-555-1212 (home), 603-555-1221 (mobile), Angela225@email.com; ConradB@email.com; and Maria Romero ("Nanny"), living at 905 Park Slope Lane, Keene, NH 03433, 603-555-2121 (home), 603-222-1515 (mobile), NannyMaria@email.com.

A. Children

Parents contract with Nanny to provide care for Dave and Larry Bradshaw ("the Children").

B. Hours and location

Nanny will care for the Children at 133 Longview Vista, Keene, NH 03431. This is a full-time job. The work hours will be between 9 a.m. and 5 p.m. Monday through Friday, unless we separately agree on a temporary schedule change.

Parents will not provide nanny with room and board as part of this agreement.

C. Start date and trial period

Nanny's first day of work will be April 1, 2010. The first 15 days will be a probationary or trial period. Parents will train Nanny during this time and give her time to learn about the Children and their care needs. At the end of that period, Parents will let Nanny know whether they wish to continue her employment. Neither Parents nor Nanny are obligated to continue the employment relationship through the entire probationary period.

D. Pay

Nanny's gross salary (before taxes) will be $600 a week. This reflects a base hourly rate of $15 per hour. If Nanny is required to do overtime, the overtime rate will be $22.50. Parents will withhold federal [*and state, if any*] income taxes from Nanny's salary.

Employment Agreement, (cont'd)

Parents have hired a payroll service, which will mail Nanny a check twice a month. Nanny will advise Parents if any problems arise with receiving these checks. Nanny will also let Parents know immediately of any expected address changes.

E. Other compensation or reimbursements

While Nanny is caring for the Children, Parents will provide food (within reasonable limits on expense and amount) for Nanny's lunch and snacks. Parents will also reimburse Nanny for gas and other money spent when caring for the Children or running household errands. However, Nanny will need to keep a record of all trips, stating the date and purpose, and provide receipts for all expenses greater than two dollars.

Parents will *not* provide room and board, nor compensate nanny for transportation or commuting costs to and from their home.

F. Vacation and holidays

Nanny will have two weeks off per year, during which time Parents will continue to pay her salary. However, at least one of these weeks must take place at the same time that the family is on vacation. Parents will discuss their vacation schedule with Nanny as far in advance as possible, in order to arrange this. And Parents ask Nanny to give at least two weeks' notice of her other week's vacation plans. If Nanny wishes to take additional, unpaid leave time, please talk to Parents about this at least one month in advance (unless it's an emergency).

At times, Parents may also ask Nanny to accompany them on vacations. This is optional, and Nanny will receive full pay plus a bonus for overnight care. [*Or describe the pay arrangement required by your state's law.*]

Employment Agreement, (cont'd)

If Parents and children take additional vacations, they will continue to pay Nanny the usual salary while away. However, Nanny will be required to visit the house at least once a day in order to take in the mail, water the plants, and handle other housesitting chores.

Nanny will receive the following holidays off with pay: New Year's Day (January 1), Independence Day, Thanksgiving, Christmas Eve Day (December 24th), Christmas Day, and New Year's Eve Day (December 31).

G. Sick leave

Nanny is entitled to three days of paid sick leave per year. If Nanny is sick for additional days, she will stay home until she is well. Nanny can choose to either deduct those days from her vacation time or take unpaid leave. On days when Nanny is staying home due to sickness, she will contact Parents by 8 a.m. at the latest.

H. Job responsibilities

Nanny's responsibilities will include the following:

Basic child care. This includes supervising and ensuring the safety of the Children at all times, engaging them in games and activities that foster their development, preparing their meals and snacks (along with Nanny's own), dressing and bathing them and changing their diapers, helping them learn personal hygiene habits (such as tooth brushing and potty training), driving them to activities or medical appointments, handling medical needs, putting Larry down for a 2 p.m. nap, imparting appropriate discipline, and cleaning up after them, including making their beds, vacuuming their rooms, and doing their laundry. Nanny will limit the children's television and video watching time to one hour per day. In addition, Parents expect Nanny to follow more detailed instructions about the house and Children that will be explained in person or put in a notebook for Nanny.

Employment Agreement, (cont'd)

Light housework. During times when Larry is napping and Dave is away on a play date or other activity, Nanny will attend to simple tasks such as washing dishes, vacuuming, or family laundry. If Nanny simply needs to rest or attend to a personal matter such as a phone call, this too is permitted, so long as it doesn't interfere with her ability to supervise the Children.

Minor errands. Parents may ask Nanny to take care of minor shopping, deliveries, or other errands during the week.

Keeping Parents informed about the Children. At the end of each day, one parent will arrive home 15 minutes before Nanny's departure time and ask for any news, good or bad—perhaps regarding the Children's progress at learning new words or a discipline or medical issue. Parents will provide Nanny with a notebook in which to log reminders of what Nanny would like to tell them.

I. **House rules**

Nanny will observe the house rules at all times. These include that Nanny will not:

- smoke, whether inside or outside the house or on a field trip with the children

- drink alcohol while on duty or use illegal drugs at any time

- entertain personal visitors in the house, unless Parents have preapproved the visit

- meet up with friends (other than fellow nannies also caring for children) while taking the Children on outings or activities

- transfer the Children to the care of any other person without the advance consent of Parents, even if it's a friend, relative, or neighbor, except in emergencies

Employment Agreement, (cont'd)

- take phone calls, emails, or text messages while the children are awake and under Nanny's supervision, or make long-distance phone calls using Parents' phone

- take the Children along on personal appointments or errands (unless it has first been cleared with Parents—for example, Parents will try to work something out if Nanny must attend a doctor appointment that can't be scheduled during nonwork hours), or

- use the house or anything in it for any personal purpose that hasn't been cleared with Parents in advance.

J. Confidentiality

Nanny may, in the course of her work, come into contact with information about the health, finances, careers, relationships, or other private matters concerning the family members or their colleagues or business clients. Nanny understands that she may not share this information with any third parties (except those who need to know, such as family physicians).

K. Review process

Parents will conduct a formal review, in which they will discuss Nanny's work and how to make any improvements, after six months, one year, and then on an annual basis.

L. At-will employment

Nanny is an at-will employee; meaning either Nanny or Parents can terminate the employment relationship at any time and for any reason that isn't illegal.

Signed

Conrad Bradshaw	*February 10, 2010*
Parent	Date
Angela Roeper	*February 10, 2010*
Parent	Date
Maria Romero	*February 10, 2010*
Nanny	Date

> **TIP**
> **You may want to add other clauses to address laws in your state.** In California, for example, employment attorney Bob King explains that, "We make sure our agreement recites the legal requirements to confirm that the nanny serves as a 'personal attendant'—that is, someone who spends at least 80% of her work time caring for a child in a private home. Under California law, a personal attendant is not entitled to the same meal periods, rest periods, and overtime pay that a regular employee would be. They're legally entitled only to federal minimum wage and overtime, which is much easier for parents to deal with." Consult with an attorney, child care agency, or state employment agency for more information.

Creating a List of Emergency Contacts

Communication with the right people at the right time is one of the best ways to minimize a crisis. For that reason, it's important that you leave your nanny or au pair a list of important phone numbers, including the following:

USA TODAY Snapshots®

Bright, healthy smiles
How parents rank their children's teeth condition:

Very good 26%
Excellent 42.5%
Good 21.9%
Poor 2.1%
Fair 7.5%

Source: Department of Health and Human Services

By David Stuckey and Alejandro Gonzalez, USA TODAY
2007

- work and mobile phone numbers for yourself and your spouse or partner

- names and phone numbers of at least two trusted friends or relatives that the nanny should try to reach if both you and your spouse and partner are unavailable in an emergency

- names and phone numbers of your immediate neighbors, in case of a neighborhood issue or the need for a quick hand (but let the nanny know which ones to call first if she needs quick help)
- names and numbers of your child's advice nurse, doctor, and even dentist (in case of something like a chipped tooth), and
- address and directions for the nearest hospital.

After creating this list, make several copies. Put one on your refrigerator, give one to your nanny, and tuck other copies into your stroller pocket, diaper bag, or other likely places.

Creating a Medical Treatment Authorization Form

If your nanny or au pair needs to take your child to the emergency room, you probably don't want to have to wait until the treatment providers can reach you in person to have your child cared for. (Of course, your nanny or au pair should be making every effort to reach you, but just in case you've turned your cell phone off and your partner is in a meeting....)

USA TODAY Snapshots®

Litany of lists

Nearly four in five Americans keep to-do lists. Types of lists kept most regularly:

Personal 73%
Work-related 66%
Household 65%
Home repairs or renovations 45%
New ideas to follow through on 36%

Note: Multiple responses allowed

Source: Windows Mobile Survey by Kelton Research of 1,004 adults, taken Nov. 27-Dec. 12. Margin of error: ± 3.1 percentage points.

By Michelle Healy and Sam Ward, USA TODAY
2008

Your doctor or local hospital may have a standard form for to use in order to deal with this potential situation. If not, below is a sample form that you can easily recreate for yourself.

Authorization for Children's Medical Treatment

Child(ren)'s name(s) and date(s) of birth: _____
_____
_____

Primary doctor's name, address, and phone number: _____
_____
_____

Health insurance provider: _____
_____
_____

Child(ren)'s medical record number(s):_____
_____
_____

Dentist's name, address, and phone number: _____
_____
_____

Dental insurance provider: _____
_____
_____

Child(ren)'s dental record number(s):_____
_____
_____

Other doctor's name, address, and phone number: _____
_____
_____

Authorization for Children's Medical Treatment, (cont'd)

Child(ren)'s allergies: _____
_____
_____

Parents' names and contact information: _____
_____
_____

Names and contact information for other adults in case parents
can't be reached: _____
_____
_____

Authorization and consent of parents

We give our authorization and consent for [*name of nanny*] to
authorize necessary medical or dental care for our child(ren)
[*name(s) of child(ren)*] _____
_____
_____
_____

Such medical treatment shall be provided upon the advice and
supervision of any physician, surgeon, dentist, or other medical
practitioner licensed to practice in the United States.

Signatures:

_____   _____
Parent   Date

_____   _____
Parent   Date

When you're done with this form, make a copy for your records, as well as a copy of your children's health insurance card, if any. Give the original form and the health insurance card copy to your nanny. Instruct her to carry these with her whenever she takes the children out of the house.

Assembling a Notebook of Other Important Instructions

No doubt there are a myriad of other things that would be useful for your nanny to know: perhaps instructions for using your fire extinguisher; the name of your veterinarian; directions to local parks and grocery stores; a list of snacks that you consider appropriate or inappropriate for your children; a list of medications that the nanny must give your child; contact information for your child's friends, especially if the nanny will be arranging play dates; where to find the water and gas shutoff valves; how to use the household security system; and so on.

USA TODAY Snapshots®

Grocery shopping for the kids

Most important factors moms consider:

Child's preference **22%**

Taste **21%**

Price **17%**

Nutritional content **27%**

Source: Ronzoni Smart Taste survey of 1,000 mothers or female guardians of children ages 5-17 conducted by Synovate. Margin of error ±3 percentage points.

By Michelle Healy and Veronica Salazar, USA TODAY 2008

As you think of these things, write them down—preferably using a computer, so you can change the document later—and put them in a notebook. Leave this in a convenient and visible place, so that the nanny can refer to it whenever she needs to.

But you'll probably also want to make clear to the nanny that it's okay to call you with questions. Absorbing all this information at once is a lot to expect, and no matter how much you put in your notebook, you'll probably forget a thing or two.

TIP

Are any of your children in school yet? If so, advise the school of your nanny's name, and comply with any of its rules allowing the nanny to pick your children up.

Day by Day: Developing and Adjusting a Routine

Y ou may be just getting used to taking care of a child yourself—and now you have to train somebody else to do so. On top of that, you have to familiarize her with your home and neighborhood. This chapter will help you through this process, from the initial training through ongoing adjustment and evaluation.

> **TIP**
> **You may end up learning from your nanny.** Susan, in Washington, DC, says: "Many parents over the years have said to me things like, 'Our nanny taught us how to put our kid to bed,' or 'Our nanny showed us how to get the sleeping baby out of the car seat and into the crib.'"

We'll cover:

- getting the room ready for a live-in
- training and monitoring
- creating a system for day-to-day communication and feedback
- preparing for and handling regular performance evaluations, and
- taking vacations together.

Although this may seem like a lot to deal with, there's a simple underlying theme here: By setting forth clear instructions at the outset, and opening the door for easy communications over the long term, you'll be able to head off many of the misunderstandings and disputes that other parents encounter.

Mints on Her Pillow? Preparing the Room for a Live-In Nanny or an Au Pair

Put some thought into preparing a room for your nanny that is both welcoming and functional—and completely private. This is as much for her happiness as it is for yours. If the nanny doesn't like spending time in her room, and its storage space is inadequate for her possessions, you'll soon find both her and her stuff taking up more space in the your house than you'd envisioned.

Here are some tips for getting the nanny's room ready:

- **Start with a total scrub down.** She'll probably notice dust and grime that you didn't (that's how it always is with someone else's house).

- **Consider repainting.** It's an inexpensive way to freshen up a room. Ideally, leave time for it to air out for a few weeks, or use nontoxic paints.

- **Empty out the space completely.** Leaving a few boxes stored in the closet or under the bed is inappropriate and can lead to your barging in at odd hours. Remember, this isn't a hotel room where she'll spend a few days of vacation—she has to operate her whole life out of this room.

USA TODAY Snapshots®

A clean sweep through the house

Rooms taking top priority during spring cleaning:

Kitchen — 37%
Living room — 19%
Bedrooms — 14%
Bathrooms — 12%
Family room — 8%

Source: International Communications Research (ICR) Omnibus telephone survey for the Soap and Detergent Association of 1,014 adults from March 1–5. Margin of error. ±3.1 percentage points.

By Mary Cadden and Marcy E. Mullins, USA TODAY
2008

- **Provide appropriate furniture.** That means a bed with sheets, blankets, and pillow cases; a chair and table or desk; a small bookshelf; a dresser (completely empty); and a wastebasket.

- **If possible, provide a TV and DVD player.** It's a nice way to help the nanny entertain herself.

- **Add decorative touches.** No need to go overboard, especially if it will take up a lot of space. But a vase of flowers or a painting on the wall shows that you care. A specially made drawing by your child is nice, too.

- **Make sure the door locks from within.** If the lock requires a key, it's okay to keep an extra one for yourself. However, warn the nanny that you have it, and make clear that you'll use it only in an emergency.

- **Create a "goody bag."** For an added welcoming touch, some parents like to put out a small basket with things like a map of the area, a gift certificate for local cups of coffee or movie tickets, snacks, a nice keychain with your house keys, and so forth.

If the nanny or au pair will have a separate bathroom, give this a good scrubbing down and put out towels and soap. While you're at it, see if you have any unused hotel shampoo and lotion to set out.

> **TIP**
>
> **If you'll be buying new things, take her along for the shopping trip.** She'll enjoy choosing colors and patterns that suit her taste. Of course, you can decide which store to go to, and it needn't be a fancy one.

If the nanny won't have a separate bathroom, make sure to specify which towel rack is hers within the bathroom she'll be using, and set out a separate cup for her toothbrush. For privacy reasons, she probably won't want to use space in your medicine cabinet, but if you can clear a drawer for her hair brush and dryer and so forth, great.

Also consider that she may want to keep certain food items separate from yours. Make some space on your kitchen shelves and in your refrigerator. Some parents even put a minirefrigerator in the nanny's room, so that she doesn't have to come padding into the kitchen for a late-night snack.

Orientation and Training

Expect to spend at least a day or two at home with the new nanny or au pair, and possibly more. You'll have lots to talk about and do, including:

- dealing with immigration, IRS, and other documents
- touring the house
- reviewing job responsibilities, including your notebook contents
- reviewing security procedures

- touring the neighborhood
- introducing your child, and
- acclimating the nanny or au pair to your child's daily routine.

> **TIP**
> **Sometimes grown-ups need naps, too.** You and the new nanny or au pair will probably both be exhausted by day's end! Make time for breaks in the middle of all this, especially if she has traveled from far away to get to your house and has jet lag.

First, the Mandatory Paperwork

Chapter 5 describes this in detail, but here's a quick list of the paperwork you'll need to take care of for a nanny (not an au pair).

- Both you and nanny will fill out Immigration Form I-9.
- You'll review the nanny's U.S. passport, work permit, or other proof of her right to work in the United States.
- If the nanny wants extra tax withheld from her paycheck, have her fill out IRS Form W-4, *Employee's Withholding Allowance Certificate.*
- If you'll be paying for health insurance, ask the nanny to complete any application forms.

If you're working with a payroll service, it may add other requirements to your list.

The House Tour Starts Here!

Start by showing your nanny or au pair around the house, explaining how its various systems work, and pointing out anything of special relevance to your child. For example, don't forget to:

- Give her a set of house as well as car keys, if she'll be driving a family car.
- Explain the alarm system, if you have one.

- Demonstrate how to use the stove, oven, microwave, and other kitchen equipment.
- Show her which baby bottles or cups, plates, and silverware your child uses.
- Open the refrigerator and cupboards and point out your child's favorite foods, as well as other food that the nanny is welcome to partake of (or not, if we're talking about your favorite organic dark chocolate), and her allotted space if she's a live-in.
- Show her where garbage and recycling go, and if she's a live-in, mention which night of the week she'll have to take out any trash in her bedroom.
- Show her which sponges, rags, and soaps you'd like her to use for cleaning up unexpected messes.
- Point out the washer, dryer, and clothesline, and explain how they work.
- If she's a live-in, demonstrate how her shower works, and point out her towel rack and personal drawer.
- Show her where Band-Aids, first aid supplies, asthma inhalers, sunscreen, and any medications that your child may need are located.
- Show her how to turn off the gas and water main in an emergency, and the location of the fuse box.
- Point out your child's favorite toys.
- Alert her to any household hazards or quirks, such as household chemicals or a window that shouldn't be opened.
- Show her around the yard, including how any gates or latches work.
- Introduce her to any pets, and explain any rules on whether they can be let outside on their own or allowed to jump on counters and couches.
- For a live-in nanny, show her not only her room, but what other household storage and other spaces are available for her use, where to get extra blankets and new sheets, and so forth.

TIP
Time to play fire drill! Every family needs an emergency plan—how to get out of the second floor if the stairwell is on fire, where to meet outside after leaving the house, and so forth. The nanny or au pair's training period is an excellent time to practice this with the kids. For more information, see the American Red Cross website, www. redcross.org (click Preparing and Getting Trained," then "Prepare—Home and Family").

The Magic Notebook: Reviewing Job Responsibilities and Instructions

Show the nanny the notebook of documents and instructions that you've created, and put a copy of your offer letter at the front of it.

Go over every item of the job description once again, this time with show and tell, such as: "We leave this curtain open a crack when he takes a nap," "Here's where toys should go at the end of the day," "There's a trick to opening this bottle of baby's medicine," or "Here are the bike and scooter, but no riding on the street, or without a helmet and knee pads."

Hand the nanny the original medical authorization form and copies of all your emergency contact information. This is a good time to give very specific instructions on how to handle an emergency, such as, "Call me

USA TODAY Snapshots®

Moms clock cleanup time

How many hours a week mothers spend cleaning the house:

1-5 hours — 61%
6-10 hours — 23%
11-15 hours — 7%
16-20 hours — 3%
More than 21 hours — 5%
None — 2%

Note: Does not equal 100% because of rounding

Source: Harris Interactive survey for Edelman of 801 mothers, March 8-13. Margin of error: ±5 percentage points

By Mary Cadden and Karl Gelles, USA TODAY 2009

before giving any medication, even if it's a baby aspirin," or "For a real emergency, call 911 first, then me, then my husband." Recommend that she program your cell phone number and your spouse's contact numbers into her mobile phone, and also memorize them, as well as your address.

Reiterate your house rules, such as "No personal visitors," "No handing the kids over to someone for an outing without checking with us first," and "No smoking."

Explain any other contents of your notebook. If you'll be asking the nanny or au pair to keep a separate log book each day, show her where this will be kept, and explain the type of entry you think is important or appropriate. Make clear that you're not asking her to write a novel, just to record key information, such as how long your child napped, what the child ate, and any unusual behavior or occurrences.

> **TIP**
> **Don't ask the nanny or au pair to take on every possible responsibility during her first week.** The first week of any job is exhausting. Think of ways to scale down expectations until she's up to speed, for example by ordering takeout instead of having her cook, or arranging play dates for your kids at other houses to give her a few hours' break.

"Don't Talk to Strangers" and Other Security Instructions

Depending on how old your nanny is, and what country or neighborhood she grew up in, she may be all but clueless about certain security procedures that you may think of as common sense. Explain to her, for example:

- **How to handle someone knocking at the door.** Explain whether she should talk to people through a window or open the door. Point out FedEx and UPS trucks if you'd like her to open the door for package deliveries.

- **How to handle your phone calls.** Should she pick up your phone, or let it go to voicemail (assuming you'll be calling her on a mobile phone)? If she will pick up, you'll most likely want her to say that you and your spouse or partner are "unavailable," rather than "not at home and it's just me here alone with the kids," and then take a message.

- **The importance of locking doors and windows at nearly all times.** Believe it or not, there are still parts of the United States and the rest of the world where this isn't necessary.

- **The need for public supervision.** Explain that when taking your children to the park, zoo, or anywhere other than your children's friends' houses, the nanny must stay close to them, at least within sight distance, at all times—including during trips into the restrooms, where it's appropriate for her to bring a small boy into the women's room.

If you have an au pair who is relatively young or unsophisticated, you may need to take these instructions one step further and talk about personal behavior. This is especially true if she'll be going out to parties or dating. As one au pair program consultant told

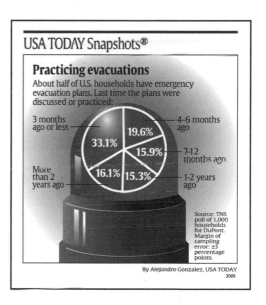

USA TODAY Snapshots®

Practicing evacuations

About half of U.S. households have emergency evacuation plans. Last time the plans were discussed or practiced:

- 3 months ago or less — 33.1%
- 4-6 months ago — 19.6%
- 7-12 months ago — 15.9%
- 1-2 years ago — 15.3%
- More than 2 years ago — 16.1%

Source: TNS poll of 1,000 households for DuPont. Margin of sampling error: ±3 percentage points.

By Alejandro Gonzalez, USA TODAY 2005

us, "I tell host families that it's your home, and the au pair is going to be part of your family, so sometimes you need to step into a parenting role and give guidance or set rules. For example, you can request that she be home every night by a certain hour—both for her safety and your peace of mind."

Arranging the Nanny's First Interactions With Your Children

At last, your nanny or au pair gets to try doing the job that she was chosen for. She has probably already met your children, but if not, introductions are in order. After that, if your child is old enough, suggest an activity such as playing or drawing in the child's bedroom.

Make clear to both the nanny and your children that you will still be in the house, and will come back in an hour.

Some kids will be perfectly happy to have someone to play with (or, in the case of infants, hold them). Others will cotton on to the fact that you are soon going to regularly leave them alone with this hitherto unknown person—and express their unhappiness loudly and clearly.

Don't jump to conclusions about whether the child "likes the nanny." At this point, a child experiencing anxiety wouldn't like Mary Poppins herself if she showed up. Be firm with your child—you're going to have to be in a few days, so you might as well start now. Close the door, but stay close enough by so that you can overhear whether the nanny is ultimately able to comfort your child or whether the situation is escalating out of control.

USA TODAY Snapshots®

Prescriptions for kids

Top five outpatient drugs prescribed for children under 18 by dollars spent, 2004:

Total spent (in millions)

Singulair (asthma)	$680
Concerta (ADHD)	$490
Strattera (ADHD)	$430
Zyrtec (allergy/ asthma)	$420
Adderall (ADHD)	$410

Source: 2004 Medical Expenditure Panel Survey, from the Agency for Healthcare Research and Quality and National Center for Health Statistics

By Tracey Wong Briggs and Marcy E. Mullins, USA TODAY 2007

The following days of your training, leave the children with the nanny for longer stretches of time. Check in periodically—or at least peek in, so your children won't see you—to see how things are going.

The Neighborhood Tour

This might be an activity you save for Day Two of the training. First, take your nanny to meet the neighbors. This is important so that they don't call the police when they see her taking your children out, and so that she knows whom to call on in an emergency.

Take your nanny and kids out for a drive, pointing out places to play, the children's friends' houses, their doctors' offices and the hospital, libraries, grocery stores, areas to avoid, and anything else the nanny should know about. Pick a few places to stop at—for example the grocery store ("Here's where they keep the goat milk, since Baby can't drink cow's milk"), and the pediatrician's office ("Park in here, and they'll validate the card").

If the nanny will be driving your children, let her do the driving on this trip. This will give you a chance to evaluate her driving skills. If she's using your car, taking the wheel right away will help her get used to it.

Also go for a walk, to show her good routes for walking with your children, if that's a regular part of their routine.

Demonstrating Your Daily Routine

The first day with the nanny or au pair might not feel "normal" to anyone. Nevertheless, try to keep as much as possible to your child's usual schedule of eating, napping, playing, being taken out for a walk, and so forth. It will be much easier for the nanny to get into the flow by watching it happen than by reading written instructions.

If discipline issues come up while both you and the nanny or au pair are with your children, count yourself lucky. She'll have a chance to watch how you deal with such situations—and therefore how you'd like them dealt with. (If your methods work, she probably won't have any argument with them!) At a certain point, the nanny will naturally start stepping in to de-escalate problems.

Talkback: Creating Communication and Feedback Systems

Being an employer for the first time is a task that almost no parent feels fully comfortable with. As Susan of Washington, DC, eloquently puts it: "Even in my work, I make a point of avoiding having to manage people, and managing someone in my home is even worse. The nanny becomes a cross between a friend, a confidante, an adviser, and someone I trust with the most precious thing in my life—my child—and yet I'm paying her, and have to hold her to standards. All I can say is, yuck!"

Even women who manage people in their professional lives tend to have similar reactions. Part of the problem is that the very things that you can't ask people at your office to do—like get you some coffee or pick up the dry cleaning—is exactly the sort of thing you may sometimes need to ask your nanny to do.

One of the best things you can do to get comfortable in this role is to open up communication channels early. Create lots of opportunities for you and the nanny or au pair to share information and talk. Give her positive reinforcement about things you notice she's done right, so that the occasional critical suggestion won't be taken as your only judgment.

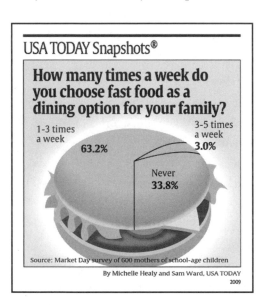

USA TODAY Snapshots®

How many times a week do you choose fast food as a dining option for your family?

1-3 times a week **63.2%**

3-5 times a week **3.0%**

Never **33.8%**

Source: Market Day survey of 600 mothers of school-age children

By Michelle Healy and Sam Ward, USA TODAY
2009

Daily Instructions

Create a system for giving the nanny or au pair any needed information or instructions at the beginning of the day, such as what food in the refrigerator should be used for everyone's lunch (and what should be left untouched, for your dinner), whether your child has a play date or medical appointment, what video you promised your child could watch that day if he or she was good, and so forth. Either set aside time to communicate this orally, designate a place for written instructions, or both.

If your "to-do list" includes things that don't necessarily need to be done that day, be clear about that. Enter deadlines, and indicate the priority in which things need to be done.

Arranging Regular Check-Ins

Based on our discussion about setting up a schedule with your nanny or au pair, you should have already figured out a time at the end of every day or at least once a week for you to touch base—that is, share information, and talk about how things are going. Although you might be hoping to hear only good news and to get on with your day, take the time to watch your nanny or au pair's demeanor and figure out whether there's anything she wants to get off her chest.

For example, if your child had a wild and wailing tantrum that day, your nanny may feel frustrated enough to tell you about it. This causes some parents to get defensive and embarrassed about their "problem" child and other parents to wonder what the nanny or au pair is doing wrong. The truth may be somewhere in between. This is your opportunity to have a constructive discussion about what might have triggered the tantrum (no nap that day?) and what methods you've found work best to stop tantrums. Encourage your nanny or au pair to let you know if the issue continues.

> **TIP**
> **Talking in person tends to work much better than via notes or email.** Even for native speakers of English, written communication is easily misunderstood, because no one sees the other person's face or tone of voice.

Also ask questions, particularly if you have noticed a change in your child's behavior or health. A new case of diaper rush, difficulty sleeping, refusal to eat vegetables—any or all of these might be indications that your nanny or au pair has changed the child's routine in a way that you might not approve of. One little well-intentioned mistake could have led to all of the above—for example, if your nanny had been using late afternoon cookies as a reward for cleaning up toys, and your child is allergic to something in those cookies or can't handle all that sugar.

> **TIP**
> **Be your child's advocate.** Like a mother lion, you have the strength to do things on behalf of your child that you'd never normally do for yourself—like laying down the law if your nanny or au pair perpetually ignores instructions or flouts house rules. Keep the focus on your child's well-being, and explain how her behavior affects that.

Finally, bring up issues that are bothering you, as directly and early as possible. Don't assume that your nanny will understand from your demeanor that you weren't happy that she decided to teach your child to read before you thought the time was right, or that she'll figure out that you regularly refold the laundry because you don't like the way she does it.

Giving Regular Feedback

In addition to the regular communication, it can be useful to set aside time once a week to take a slightly broader view. This is particularly important if your caregiver is an au pair, for whom a full-scale performance review isn't really appropriate given her youth and the short length of her stay. You can style these meetings as something innocuous, like the "schedule review" for the upcoming week—then, as you're planning what's ahead, gently mention that you'd also like her to focus on something like "finding effective ways to redirect Junior's attention before an angry spell turns into a tantrum," or "winding down to more quiet activities before naptime."

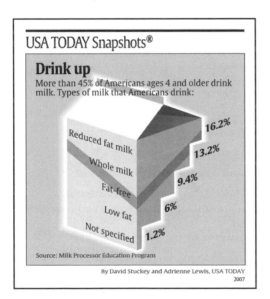

USA TODAY Snapshots®

Drink up

More than 45% of Americans ages 4 and older drink milk. Types of milk that Americans drink:

Reduced fat milk 16.2%
Whole milk 13.2%
Fat-free 9.4%
Low fat 6%
Not specified 1.2%

Source: Milk Processor Education Program

By David Stuckey and Adrienne Lewis, USA TODAY
2007

Of course, if your suggestions can't wait, it's important to find ways to give immediate feedback that feel comfortable to you and the nanny or au pair. Take a deep breath, and say something like, "Can we talk about preparing Junior's lunch? The microwave can make food really hot in some areas, and I noticed him crying this morning from a hot bite. I've found that it works best to stir the microwave food carefully and taste it before feeding him. Would you try that from now on?"

Once you see that your nanny or au pair is able to accept advice, you'll be better able to address larger issues. Whatever you do, however, don't put off dealing with areas of concern until you're at the breaking point. If you're lashing out with something like "If you didn't always wear those flimsy flip flops and talk on your cell phone at the park, maybe you could have run after Junior in time to stop him from jumping into the fountain!" you've let a problem go on too long.

If you've hired an experienced nanny, you may find it difficult to reassert control after an initial period during which you deferred to the nanny because she was the biggest expert on child rearing of anyone in the house. Your efforts may actually confuse your nanny. At the outset, you smiled with relief when she took the initiative and decided what was best for your child—perhaps that your baby was ready for solid food—but now you look unhappy after she potty trains your child without consulting you. You'll need to thank the nanny for her willingness to take on extra responsibility, then explain—possibly more than once that you'd like her to discuss matters with you before making any significant parenting decisions or instituting any major changes in your child's routine.

Conducting Formal Reviews

This section is for employers of nannies only (not employers of au pairs). Everyone hates the idea of a job review, no matter which side of the table they're sitting on. But done right, a review can be a satisfying time to acknowledge what the nanny is doing well, clear the air about things that either of you is dissatisfied with, and make plans for improvement.

If you've set a probationary or trial period with your nanny, do your first formal review at the end of it. To organize your thoughts, go back to your original job description and create a new document that breaks it up, topic by topic. Then either give numerical ratings to your nanny's performance or write down comments on how well she's doing at each particular task.

In addition, think about how the nanny is doing at more abstract parts of the job, like developing a positive relationship with your child and with you and helping your child learn and grow.

Schedule a time to meet when your children won't be present. Start by thanking the nanny for her hard work and acknowledging some of the best parts of her performance, like "We're so happy that you and Junior seem to have so much fun together." Then review the contents of your document, and give a copy to the nanny to keep. When you need to deliver criticism, keep it constructive, by explaining how she can improve on this matter. (Unless, of course, you plan to fire her, in which case there is no more time for improvement!)

Also give the nanny a turn to express her thoughts. Ask her whether there's anything you can do to make her job easier.

It's possible, of course, that this is the end of the line, and you'll be terminating your employment relationship. If so, you can shorten the meeting, and forgo the written evaluation. Just keep it businesslike, for example by explaining, "We've appreciated your efforts and have enjoyed getting to know you, but this just isn't working out." We'll talk more about firing a nanny in Chapter 12.

Taking Vacations Together

Once you've found a nanny you know and trust, you may decide that having her along on your international tour, beach vacation, or camping trip would help both you and the kids have a more enjoyable time. If you have more than two children, it means everyone has a hand to hold as you cross unfamiliar streets. And the nanny may indeed be willing to do this—though you'll need to negotiate a few matters in advance.

The first issue is pay (unless you have an au pair, in which case the usual stipend is fine). Some parents mistakenly think the nanny should be paid less, because the parents will be covering all the costs of her transportation, hotel rooms, and food. Better think again on this one— the nanny didn't choose this vacation, and she won't ever really get to fully relax and enjoy it. In fact, she may be taking care of your kids more hours a day than usual, especially if you ask her to sleep in their room (or tent) and spend evenings with the kids while you're out at a nice restaurant. As Shylah, a former au pair and professional nanny says, "A vacation is not a vacation if you're always around the family; it feels as though you're working 24/7."

Plan to pay the nanny at least her weekly salary. Adjusting it upwards a bit for the extra hours is even better (and may be required by your state's law, as discussed earlier; for example, California requires her to be paid for any extra travel time). Higher pay will also make the nanny less resentful if you get back from dinner late. Also make very clear ahead of time how many hours the nanny will be expected to work, whether she will indeed be sharing a room with the kids, and when she'll be given breaks. Don't forget the breaks—she'll need some time to get away and be by herself. Of course, if she goes out for time on her own, she'll have to cover the costs.

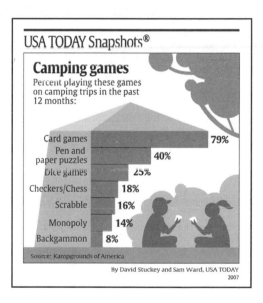

USA TODAY Snapshots®

Camping games
Percent playing these games on camping trips in the past 12 months:

Card games	79%
Pen and paper puzzles	40%
Dice games	25%
Checkers/Chess	18%
Scrabble	16%
Monopoly	14%
Backgammon	8%

Source: Kampgrounds of America

By David Stuckey and Sam Ward, USA TODAY 2007

A less tangible but equally important issue to talk about in advance is who will take the lead on disciplinary matters when you're all together. Shylah says, "I went to Disneyworld with the first family I joined in the United States. There were some awkward times, because when the parents are around, you're never sure what your role is. Children usually behave very differently for their parents than for their nannies. The behavior techniques I use as a nanny never work as well when parents are around, and children usually play up for their parents to get attention."

It's impossible to come up with a neat solution, but talking about your approach ahead of time at least avoids major misinterpretations of each others' signals. It may be easiest for you to tell the nanny that on group excursions, you'll be the main one in charge, but may ask the nanny to step in or take one or more of the children and distract or entertain that one slightly apart from the rest of the group.

Taking Trips Without the Kids

Once your kids are old enough, and you've found a nanny whom you trust completely, you might want to take a vacation that's just for grownups. Or, a business trip might require hiring the nanny to stay with the little ones. Although leaving the kids alone with a nanny (or other babysitter) can cause parents a lot of anxiety, it often turns out to be harder on the parents than the kids.

> **CAUTION**
> **Don't leave the kids alone with an au pair.** She may still be young herself, and taking a vacation without her certainly won't enhance her experience of the United States. If you must leave town, you might want to hire an additional babysitter to share the load, or ask a friend to sleep over.

Proper planning is, of course, critical. You don't want to have the preschool refuse to turn your child over to the nanny, or for her not to know which doctor to call when your child loses the asthma inhaler. Here's how to make it work.

Notify All Appropriate People

You may have already introduced your nanny to the important people in your child's world, but an impending trip is a good time to remind people of who she is. Advise them of the dates that you'll be away and the fact that she'll be the primary caregiver. People to talk to include your:

- immediate neighbors (but don't send out an email to a neighborhood listserv if you don't know and trust everyone on it)
- teachers
- close family members

- friends with whom your child might have a play date while you're away, and

- your alarm company, if you have one (and don't forget to give the nanny any passwords).

TIP

Written your will yet? Actually, you're probably in no more danger traveling than battling your daily commute, but now's a good time to take care of this detail. Naming a guardian for your children is especially important, so that someone will be available to step in and relieve the nanny from duty if the worst happens. You can write a will online at Nolo (www.nolo.com) and then print it out; or you can purchase and download a simple will form to your hard drive that you can complete and print (type "Quick and Legal Will Book" into Nolo's home page search box).

Arrange Communication Methods

Many parents find it's helpful to arrange a set time every day to check in. But in case your nanny needs to reach you at other times, be sure to leave a complete itinerary (including flight or cruise numbers), and not only cell phone numbers but any alternate numbers of hotels or friends with whom you'll be staying. And make sure your nanny understands any changes in time zones, unless you want to hear about your child's good report card at 2 a.m.

Prepare the House

Stock the fridge, pay any bills (particularly from the electricity company), and walk around to remind yourself of any hazards you should remove (or warn of) or locked areas to which your nanny will need a key. Remind her (and probably yourself) of the location of gas and water shutoff valves and fire extinguishers. Leave enough cash for her to pay for normal activities with the kids and for any additional food or supplies (but set ground rules, and ask her to keep receipts).

Provide Detailed Instructions for the Evenings

If your nanny isn't a live-in, she probably hasn't spent whole nights with your children. Give her a detailed schedule of evening routines, bedtimes, and any other information she'll find helpful (who's scared of the dark, what stuffed animals must be tucked in alongside a certain child, and so forth).

Also reiterate your house rules, just in case she thinks overnight stays constitute an exceptional circumstance. If, for example, your "no visitors" and "no alcohol" rule extends to evenings (and they should), those are important messages to convey to the nanny.

Ask Friends and Family to Check In

Some unannounced visits from familiar friends or family aren't a bad idea, just to make sure everything is going smoothly. Even having someone call your house to ask whether the nanny needs any help can be a welcome sign of support. Taking care of even one child is a big task for just one person!

How to Keep a Nanny You Like

There's nothing like having a good nanny. Jackie, a mom in Northern California, for example, says, "I used to love coming home and seeing my children completely engaged in some project, like making an animal village out of rocks in the sandbox. Our nanny could do the most amazing things with minimal household supplies. My kids still say things like, 'Do you remember those fun things she showed us how to do with shaving cream?'"

Such a nanny should not be taken for granted. True, her own good heart will lead her to become increasingly attached to your family, in particular to your child, which may keep her there even in the face of frustration or better job offers. But there's no question that a good nanny has other options and may even receive unsolicited and potentially irresistible offers. In fact, the median job tenure in the child care industry is only 2.7 years. Annual turnover tends to run between 30% and 40%, which is nearly twice the rate as in other industries.

USA TODAY Snapshots®

What makes workers happy?

Personal satisfaction defining who I am	27%
Just having a job at all	24%
Work/personal life balance	14%
Co-workers and clients	12%

Source: SnagAJob.com survey of 1,006 employees. Margin of error ±3 percentage points

By Jae Yang and Sam Ward, USA TODAY
2009

So, if you like your nanny, make sure you show it, in both word and deed. Here are some hints, drawn from actual mothers' and nannies' experiences.

The Bare Minimum: How to Keep Your Nanny in the Job

Having found and successfully hired a nanny you like, you're doubtless planning to be a considerate and fair employer, if only to make sure that she doesn't feel exploited and want to leave. And, not incidentally, you probably know that the way you interact with your nanny will be noticed by even young children, who will draw conclusions about how one should treat this person and any other adult in a business situation. Just as they mimic your table manners, your children will copy your tone of voice and body language, not to mention the patience and respect (or lack thereof) you accord your nanny.

Even if you see your nanny for a few minutes every day, certain actions—or inactions—convey distinct messages. Remember to consider how things might look from the nanny's point of view, using the cautions below.

- **Pay her on time.** She shouldn't have to ask and may feel embarrassed if she has to. (Another good reason to hire a payroll service.)

- **Don't foist basic parenting tasks onto the nanny.** Some parents practically ignore the kids' needs until the nanny shows up in the morning, leaving her to cope with the chaos. That's not entirely fair. Yes, you're busy, but as Trina, a nanny in Chicago says, "We're talking about their kids! It used to shock me when the parents would hand me the baby with a poopy diaper. And I don't mean the baby had just happened to poop in the minutes before the parents left for work, that diaper had been poopy for a long time."

USA TODAY Snapshots®

What employees want
What aspect is important when your employer communicates with you? Top responses:

Giving insights on how to be more effective — 52%
Showing how to fit into the company's vision — 47%
Explaining the company's vision — 45%
Engaging on a personal level — 41%

Note: Multiple responses allowed
Source: Jack Morton Worldwide Experiential Marketing Global Consumer Response survey of 1,625 workers and job seekers conducted by Sponsorship Research International. Margin of error ±2 percentage points.

By Jae Yang and Marcy E. Mullins, USA TODAY 2006

- **Don't invade the nanny's privacy.** She has a life of her own and may be understandably unwilling to give up her time on short notice or to share details of what she does and who she sees when she's not at your house. Unless you have evidence that your nanny's private activities are affecting your children, be alert to and respect her boundaries. (It's okay, and even recommended, however, to ask her how her day went.)

- **Don't make her a second-class citizen in your house.** Some parents have been known to put out separate utensils for the nanny, or have her eat separate food, sometimes even at a separate table. They may try to justify this with, "Well, she's from a third-world country; this is what she's used to." Whether the nanny lives with you or simply eats some meals with you, such second-class treatment is tacky and will lead to resentment. And don't forget that Diana Spencer worked as a nanny for an American family before she married Prince Charles—the family's surprise at discovering her lineage and prospects is chronicled in the book *The Diana I Knew: The Story of My Son's Nanny Who Became the Princess of Wales*, by Mary Robertson (Piatkus Books,1998).

- **Pay overtime when it's due.** As discussed in Chapter 4, federal law requires you to pay one and a half times the nanny's usual hourly rate for any week in which she works more than 40 hours (even if she's on an otherwise fixed salary). In some states (such as California, Alaska, and Nevada), you must also pay overtime on any day that the nanny works more than a certain number of hours, usually eight (but 12 in Colorado). These rules don't apply to live-in nannies.

- **Don't let the kids treat your nanny like their servant.** The employer-nanny relationship is a tough one for many parents to get used to, especially in a society where making someone your servant is considered disrespectful. Yet the nanny isn't a mere friend who shows up at your house—you pay her, and you get to call most of the shots. But your kids don't, and letting them think they can order the nanny around will only lead to spoiled kids and a disgruntled nanny. Reyna, a nanny in Tacoma, says, "One boy in the house where I worked as a live-in would give me orders, like, 'Get me a glass of milk!' I'd gently remind him that he was old enough (11 years) to get one for himself, which I'd often heard his parents tell him. But then once or twice the mother heard me, and decided to win points by pouring him some milk herself. I felt this undermined my authority and contributed to the boy's increasingly entitled behavior."

- **Don't expect the nanny to babysit your friend's kids for free.** As Michelle, a former nanny in Wisconsin explains, "I used to feel very put upon when the doorbell would ring, and next thing I know the mother was telling me, 'This is little Susie, her mother and I are going out for manicures, see you later!'" Caring for extra kids should be negotiated in advance and compensated appropriately.

USA TODAY Snapshots®

Most stay at first job less than 2 years
How long did you stay at the first full-time job you took after graduating college?

Less than one year	36%
One to two years	42%
Three to four years	13%
More than five years	4%
Haven't worked since college	5%

Source: Experience.com "2006 Life After College" study of 320 college graduates.

By Jae Yang and Robert W. Ahrens, USA TODAY 2006

- **If she's "one of the family," make that a two-way street.** In other words, if you expect the nanny to do things outside her job description like gift shop for your friends or change the schedule on short notice, be ready to do the same things for her in a pinch.

- **Support the nanny's discipline of your children.** Let's say, for example, you've told the nanny that your child must make his bed and neaten his room before going out to play in the morning. If he doesn't do it, you don't let him advance to the next planned activity. Suppose the nanny tells you that she had to skip the morning trip to the park when your child refused to do his chores. When you're back on the scene on the weekend, if you overlook his failure to straighten his room and let the day proceed as scheduled, you're sending a not-so-subtle signal that you disagree with the nanny's approach. Most children will try again to disregard the nanny's instructions, and sooner or later you will have to deal with the consequences (a demoralized nanny and a difficult child). Remind your child that the nanny is the boss, and follow through by refusing to undermine her appropriate discipline.

CAUTION
When the nanny isn't the boss. All parents should be separately teaching their children what constitutes inappropriate behavior by adults, and reminding the children to come to them if any adult ever touches them inappropriately, becomes violent, or says, "Don't tell your mommy or daddy about this."

Celebrities Who've Been Sued by Their Nannies

Maybe you can't pay Hollywood nanny rates, but look on the bright side—you're less likely to get mired in disputes of outsize proportions, like the following:

- **Heather Mills**, former wife of Sir Paul McCartney, was sued by a former nanny in 2008. The nanny claimed sex discrimination and intimidation, alleging that she'd been made to work until midnight and do inappropriate tasks like give a naked Ms. Mills a spray tan and blow dry her hair early in the morning.

- **Lisa Marie Presley** was sued in August 2009 by her "postpartum caregiver," claiming she herself was suffering from "transferred postpartum depression," having not been given meal breaks or overtime pay during the 24-hours-a-day, seven-day-a-week schedule she was forced to work. But Ms. Presley claims she paid the nanny the sum of $650 per day.

- Also in 2009 (when the recession must have been making everyone penny conscious), **Robert De Niro** was sued by a former nanny claiming the actor stiffed her out of $40,000 in overtime pay and fired her when she complained and that she never got her ten promised days of vacation.

We could go on.

A Little Extra: How to Make Your Nanny Happy

Don't wait for the holidays to give your nanny gifts and other forms of thanks. Even small gestures, at any time of year, can remind her that you recognize her hard work. Audrey, a nanny in New Jersey, says, "I loved it when the mom, who worked at home, would come back from her early morning errands with a coffee for me. She knew that the kids were always at their crankiest right around then, and that I could use the pick-me-up."

Here are some other ways to acknowledge all your nanny does for you:

- **Say thank you, more often than might seem normal.** Nannies (and pretty much anyone else) are happy to hear "thank you" as often as you can say it (but don't overdo it—a rote "Oh, thank you!" dozens of times a day will soon become meaningless). For example, Shylah, a former au pair and now a nanny in New Zealand, says, "As an au pair, I don't ever recall being thanked. It would have made a big difference because I would have felt more important and welcome. Nannying is better, I get thanked every day, for small things such as cleaning the kitchen, and it makes me want to do extra things to help out." Writing a short thank you note after the nanny has done something special is a great way to show you really mean it.

USA TODAY Snapshots®

Employees want to make a difference

What do you think is the most important factor in job success? Top factors:

Using my talents to make a difference	36%
Financial success	29%
New opportunities	13%
Creating new solutions to existing problems	9%
Being able to give back to my community and society at large	9%

Source: Ace Hardware survey of 1,059 adults 18 and older conducted by Impulse Research. Margin of error ±3 percentage points.

By Jae Yang and Adrienne Lewis, USA TODAY 2007

- **Let the nanny knows your child cares about her.** If, for example, your child asks for the nanny when she's not there, or says he or she "loves" her, tell the nanny. You may have to get over your own feelings of being threatened by this—that is, by the nanny becoming too much like a second mom—but, after years of mothers worrying over this very issue, there's virtually no evidence of it leading to actual problems. In the meantime, you'll make the nanny's day.

- **Celebrate her birthday.** The nanny may well have attended her share of kids' birthday parties by now, so she deserves at least a little something on her own birthday. (Check the date from her employment documents, and mark it in your personal calendar.) This is definitely one to get the kids involved in, if they're old enough to understand birthdays. Have them plan in secret, perhaps the night before, and make her birthday cards, little gifts, or even a cake if they're old enough to stir.

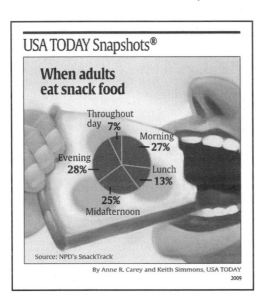

USA TODAY Snapshots®

When adults eat snack food

Throughout day 7%
Morning 27%
Evening 28%
Lunch 13%
25% Midafternoon

Source: NPD's SnackTrack

By Anne R. Carey and Keith Simmons, USA TODAY
2009

- **Stock your house with snacks she'll enjoy.** Ask the nanny what she likes, and invite her to help herself. That doesn't, of course, mean setting forth an endless array of sweet or junky temptations, particularly if that's not what you're teaching your kids to eat. But she might appreciate some nice seasonal fresh fruit, yogurt, cheese and crackers, her favorite flavors of tea, or bagels.

- **Stick to the job description.** A nanny who discovers, for example, that she's a housekeeper with some child care duties on the side is likely to quit. If you must change her job description, for example by adding tasks to her list, be conscious of when you're doing so, ask for her agreement, and compensate her accordingly, either at the time or when considering a raise or bonus.

TIP
Having another child is a major change to the job description! Don't expect the nanny to take on this new duty without a pay raise. There's no need to double her pay (that's one of the benefits of having a nanny). Learn the going rate for two children in your area.

- **Give raises or bonuses, if possible.** For details on the timing and appropriate amounts, see "Planning Ahead: Raises and Bonuses," in Chapter 4. Of course, if you aren't satisfied with your nanny's performance, giving a raise or bonus is not required—but in this chapter, we're assuming you'd like your nanny to stick around, and paying her well is the best way to ensure that. And don't forget that you can give cash bonuses or small gifts at any time; no need to wait until the end of the year!

- **Ask her to lunch or dinner occasionally.** Unless the nanny already lives with you, inviting her to share a meal—especially if it's one where the kids aren't there—is valuable for a variety of reasons. It's a treat for her, it's a nice way of saying thank you, and it's a good opportunity for you and her to bond and have some adult conversation. Even if all your feedback systems are in place (as discussed in Chapter 10), there's nothing like a long, casual chat to draw someone out.

USA TODAY Snapshots®

What is your favorite cookie?

Chocolate chip **53%**

Peanut butter **16%**

15% Oatmeal

11% Sugar/ shortbread

5% Other

Source: Impulse Research for Downtown Cookie Co. survey of 1,033 adults

By Anne R. Carey and Sam Ward, USA TODAY 2009

- **Offer other perks.** These don't have to cost extra money. For example, if you have transferable frequent-flier miles you don't plan to use, extra fruit from your tree, or friends who will give her a discount at their business, this might help compensate for a less-than-stellar salary. An extra day off is always welcome. And if you have bags of clothes and other goods that you're about to give to charity, invite her to see whether she'd like anything in them first. (You'd do the same thing for a close friend or relative, so why not your nanny?)

12

Coping with Trouble, and Ending the Nanny Relationship

Even a nanny who feels like part of the family will have to leave someday, either because your kids have grown or because it's time for her to move on with her own life. And then, there are the nannies who never become part of the family—in fact, become problems that you need to deal with.

Sometimes, your child's age will make a difference in whether the nanny is a good match. Susan, of Washington, DC, says, "My daughter's first nanny just loved my daughter when she was a baby. But it turned out she wasn't so great with toddlers—she was way more interested in keeping the house neat. By the time my daughter was 18 months old or so, I would set up finger paints or Play Doh, which I knew my daughter could be completely engaged with for at least half an hour. Then I'd go upstairs to work, and within ten minutes, the nanny would have cleaned it all up. To her, that was chaos. I finally realized she was no longer the right person for the job."

In this chapter, we'll help you through the end stages of your relationship with a nanny, including how to:

- Keep an eye out for potential problems with the nanny's behavior—without resorting to nanny cams.
- Fire a nanny when necessary.
- Handle the break with a nanny whose behavior was fine, but who leaves for other reasons.

TIP
This chapter addresses primarily nannies, not au pairs.
However, you should review the sections on watching for signs of trouble, below. If problems do arise with your au pair, your local coordinator will be your primary contact. She should both help you resolve difficulties and, if need be, arrange for your au pair's return to her home country. Your contract with your au pair agency most likely also permits you to bring in a replacement au pair at a reduced cost.

Watching for Signs of Trouble

Everyone has a bout of laziness or a bad day once in awhile, and nannies are no exception. But if your nanny shows any signs of ongoing difficult, dishonest, or otherwise negative behavior, you'll need to act fast. She has too much control of your house and your children for you to indulge in even a moment of procrastination.

Useful Monitoring Techniques

There's no need to become endlessly suspicious, but the steps below will help you either unveil a problem nanny early on or reassure yourself that all is going well.

- **Drop in unexpectedly.** Especially at the beginning of your nanny's work tenure, think up excuses to return home at odd times. A forgotten purse or lunch, an unexpected afternoon off, or other such excuses work well. Or ask a friend or neighbor to do the same thing. An experienced nanny will take this in stride—she

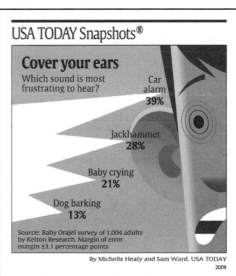

USA TODAY Snapshots®

Cover your ears
Which sound is most frustrating to hear?

Car alarm **39%**

Jackhammer **28%**

Baby crying **21%**

Dog barking **13%**

Source: Baby Orajel survey of 1,004 adults by Kelton Research. Margin of error margin ±3.1 percentage points

By Michelle Healy and Sam Ward, USA TODAY
2009

  may even know perfectly well what you're up to, but will understand that any vigilant parent does the same thing.

- **Count the diapers.** Check how many diapers there are in your child's drawer at the beginning and end of a day. Is your nanny using, on average, as many as you did? Or is your child spending too much of the day in wet or soiled diapers—or worse yet, not getting enough liquids? (You might check on the reduction in milk or formula levels, too.) If your nanny is young or inexperienced, you may simply need to tell her how often it's appropriate to check the child's diapers.

- **Keep an eye on petty cash and valuables.** In this case, you're hoping to see that the amount stays the same, instead of dropping! Don't leave temptations like jewelry or credit cards sitting around. Keep an eye on other household supplies, too. Cora, a mom in Portland, Oregon, says, "After our former nanny's first week on the job, I started noticing that the levels in our shampoo and soap bottles were lower, and we seemed to be going through toilet paper awfully quickly. I couldn't really prove anything, but I had to trust that the fact that so many things just didn't look right to me meant trouble; so we let her go."

USA TODAY Snapshots®

Do you feel vulnerable to identity theft?

Yes **53%**

No **31%**

15% Neither yes/no

1% Refused to answer

Source: KRC Research for Fellowes survey of 1,002 adults May 8-11

By Anne R. Carey and Sam Ward, USA TODAY
2009

- **Check your bank and credit card statements carefully.** The sad truth is that someone spending time in your home is well poised to commit identity theft. Many thieves start small, for example by writing a check for a few dollars from the back of your checkbook. Then, when they see you haven't noticed, they may drain your account. Or, a thief may use your name and Social Security number to open new credit card accounts in your name. (If you don't already, it's worth regularly checking your credit reports, which you can do for free at www.annualcreditreport.com. And keep your Social Security card and number well hidden.)

- **Once a day or so, look carefully at your child when he or she has no clothes on.** Though it doesn't happen often, bruises and other signs of abuse can be hidden by a nanny who is the only one to change the child in and out of pajamas every day.

- **If you notice signs of injuries, ask how they happened.** Every child gets some bumps and scrapes in the course of playing or discovering the world. But if your nanny gives vague answers about what exactly happened, like "Oh, I think she fell off something," or answers that don't make sense, for example because you know your child never climbs on a certain object or isn't even walking yet, you may have a problem.

- **Be alert to your child's behavior changes.** Unusual clinginess, anxiety, fear of other people, or new phobias could all be signs of mistreatment—or at best, a nanny who isn't able to keep your child to the usual routine of naps and other activities.

- **Take a look at your car regularly, if the nanny drives it.** Ask about any new scrapes or dings. Check the odometer—does it reflect the driving you expect and authorized?

- **Keep your radar up.** It's amazing—and a bit disturbing how many parents who've had to fire a nanny will say something like, "I had a feeling something wasn't right; I should have trusted my intuition." If you think something is up, ask the nanny questions, remind her of your expectations, and investigate using the steps described above. You don't need direct proof of problems. If, for example, your nanny is regularly late or seems disinterested in the child's birthday or recovery from an illness,

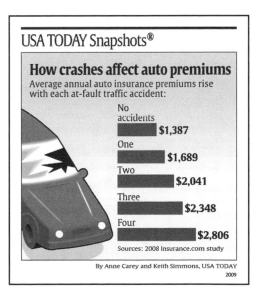

USA TODAY Snapshots®

How crashes affect auto premiums
Average annual auto insurance premiums rise with each at-fault traffic accident:

No accidents — **$1,387**
One — **$1,689**
Two — **$2,041**
Three — **$2,348**
Four — **$2,806**

Sources: 2008 Insurance.com study

By Anne Carey and Keith Simmons, USA TODAY 2009

those alone are strong indications that she's just not into this job. When in doubt, let her go and find someone else. You want a nanny you feel comfortable with and confident in.

Of course, some problems will be obvious. For example, a nanny who is getting into arguments with your children will not be able to paste smiles on their faces when you're about to step through the front door. Susan, in Washington, DC, remembers: "Our second nanny was a woman with whom I had a lot in common. The boundaries between friend and employer got blurred, in a bad way. One day, for example, I found her lounging on my bed picking her toenails. But the final straw was when I came home to find my daughter under the dining room table crying, while the nanny was on the couch casually reading a magazine. I said, 'You know what, you don't have to come back tomorrow, I've made other plans.'"

> ### At least the nanny won't be taking your last name!
>
> In 19th-century England, servants were considered such integral parts of the household that they routinely adopted their employers' surnames.

Should You Install a Nanny Camera?

You've probably heard of these little spy devices: hidden cameras stashed anywhere from plants to teddy bears to mantle clocks, meant to reveal the nanny's activities and behavior during the hours when you aren't home. In a high percentage of cases where parents install such a camera, they end up discovering justification to fire the nanny.

But, as with so many statistics, there are different ways to read this. At first, it sounds like most nannies are up to no good. But if that were the case, wouldn't there be more firings and prosecutions? Violence prevention expert Gavin de Becker, in his book *Protecting the Gift*, points out: "Most parents who've decided to install a hidden camera already wanted to fire the babysitter or nanny but didn't have the courage to do it without proof." If you're already suspicious, he says, trust your intuition, stop conducting this "high-stakes experiment with [your] own baby," and "get rid of the babysitter."

Some parents have wondered, given this analysis, whether it wouldn't be more fair to simply install a camera at the beginning—maybe even telling the nanny it's there. However, getting cameras hidden in all the areas of your house can be impossible, and because the tapes don't show any problems in the few areas you can see, you'd create a false sense of security. (And are you really going to devote the hours it would take to review all the tapes, most of which will show innocent or minimal activity?) Also consider these words by Shylah, a nanny in New Zealand: "I wouldn't work for a family who told me they'd installed a nanny cam. There's a feeling of trust that needs to be present between nanny and parents. Also, knowing you're on camera makes most people uncomfortable and self-conscious and you therefore behave differently than usual. During the first few weeks of a new nanny job, it's important to be strict and set clear boundaries. Once the children are behaving appropriately, you lighten up and have more fun. If I knew I was being filmed I probably wouldn't be as firm as I usually am, and then the behavior of the children could be difficult to manage throughout the rest of the job. On the other hand, I'd rather they tell me than hide the camera! I know many nannies

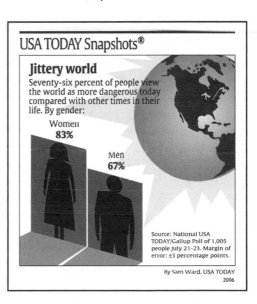

USA TODAY Snapshots®

Jittery world

Seventy-six percent of people view the world as more dangerous today compared with other times in their life. By gender:

Women
83%

Men
67%

Source: National USA TODAY/Gallup Poll of 1,005 people July 21-23. Margin of error: ±3 percentage points.

By Sam Ward, USA TODAY 2006

who check the entire house for cameras during the first week of work. It's pretty easy to hunt for them when you're cleaning."

Firing a Nanny for Behavior Reasons

If you think you need to fire your nanny, start moving quickly now. The first thing to do, even before you've fully investigated and thought through your decision, is to start lining up backup or replacement care. That's because, when you let her go, you may want it to go into effect immediately, as part of the at-will employment we discussed in

Chapter 9. Depending on the reasons for the firing and her level of maturity, you may not want her showing up the next morning or spending time alone that with your child. It may feel a little dishonest in the meantime, but you've really got no choice.

> **TIP**
>
> **Did you sign an employment agreement with your nanny promising to give notice before terminating her?** This book did not recommend that you do so, but you might have entered into such an agreement if you used a nanny agency. Check the language of that agreement—even if it requires advance notice of termination, it was probably only for cases where the termination wasn't "for cause." You're firing your nanny for a reason.

Next, get in touch with your payroll service, if you're using one. Find out its procedures for cutting a final check—you'll ideally want to hand the check to your nanny on her way out the door. (In fact, this is legally required in some states, though others give you up to a week, or until the next scheduled payday.) Of course, if her behavior was truly egregious, you should fire her right away and tell her you'll send the check promptly.

There's no need to give her any severance pay, unless you want to; you owe her only for the time that she has worked. If she has accrued unused vacation time, your state's law may require you to pay her for that.

If you have children in school, wait until the nanny has picked them up for the last time, and then immediately advise the school to take her off their list.

If the nanny's behavior doesn't present any risk to your house or child—for example, she's simply late every day or you can't stand the way she leaves dirty dishes around the house—you can wait until you've organized things like backup care and the final check, then pick a day to deliver the bad news. Telling her at the end of the day is best, so that she's not alone with your child while she's angry and hurt. In fact, make sure your child is out of the room when you deliver the news—though they should later be given an opportunity to say goodbye.

Keep the conversation businesslike. State what part of her behavior was not working for you and your child. There's no need to be mysterious about this, and you want her to improve for the sake of future children. Try not to vent your anger and frustration. Of course, make clear that there's no room for argument—your decision has been made, and now it's just a matter of moving forward.

Ask for your house keys and any other personal possessions back, and give her a chance to get hers.

If your nanny is a live-in, of course, all of this gets more complicated. If she doesn't have someplace to stay locally, you may need to make arrangements for her to stay at a local motel for a few nights. Then plan to have her come back on another day to move her possessions. Taking a day or two off work during the transition might be wise. If the nanny's home is far away, be prepared to pay her bus, plane, or U-Haul fare— you don't want to find her camped out in your local park.

> ⓘ **CAUTION**
> **Be sensitive in explaining the break to your child.** If your child has bonded with the nanny, he or she may not care whether she's been stealing the shampoo and will be upset by the sudden news of her departure. (Children less than two years old, however, may take the transition in stride.) Also, as with divorce situations, your child might worry that he or she is somehow at fault for the breakup. Allow plenty of time to talk this through—*after* the nanny has left. (Don't prepare your child ahead of time—you probably already know how often children will spill the beans!)

Working Nannies Fight Stereotypes

The career field still is fighting cliches: Nannies are attractive, sex-crazed, man-stealing vultures. Nannies are magical beings with British accents. Nannies are thieves and bullies kept under control by "nanny cams." Nannies are the enemy.

"It's incredibly sad when stories like these take attention away from the hard work these women do by propagating a myth," says Nicola Kraus, who cowrote the best-selling novel *The Nanny Diaries* with Emma McLaughlin.

Hollywood's portrayal of nannies in film and television hasn't exactly been flattering, except for Julie Andrews, who starred as a nanny in two movie classics: *Mary Poppins* and *The Sound of Music.* More sinister caregivers include Rebecca De Mornay's homicidal psycho in 1992's *The Hand that Rocks the Cradle* to the all-too-perfect Paz Vega in 2004's *Spanglish* to the nasally voiced, annoying Fran Drescher in the 1990s sitcom "The Nanny."

On a much-talked-about episode of "Desperate Housewives," Lynette (Felicity Huffman) fired her dream nanny (Marla Sokoloff) because her husband found her attractive.

"People have this misconception that nannies are gorgeous creatures, and for the most part, they are not," says Annie Davis, president of the Seattle-based National Alliance of Professional Nanny Agencies. "Some people would just as soon not have a really attractive woman in the house because that situation could develop.

"But it doesn't happen as much as the media says it happens. Nannies are there to take care of the children, not seduce the husband."

Think "Supernanny" or "Nanny 911," not *Playboy,* and that's the average profile of an American nanny, says Pat Cascio, president of the Houston-based International Nanny Association.

"I'm personally leery of placing women under 30 as nannies because of life changes; it may be a transitional job to them," she says.

Working Nannies Fight Stereotypes, (cont'd)

"Whereas people in their 30s have chosen this as a career and enjoy working with children, caring for them, watching the child grow."

The average nanny has a college degree, and many are former teachers or pediatric nurses, Cascio says.

Boston-based Michelle LaRowe, the 2004 International Nanny Association Nanny of the Year, says she has turned down offers of more money to work for famous families because of the relationship she has established with her charges, 6-year-old twin boys she has cared for since they were 10 days old.

"I love my job. You can't put a price tag on that," says LaRowe, 29. "You become emotionally connected to the families; you become part of the family."

LaRowe says her colleagues are fed up with the media focus on nannies gone wild.

"As in any other industry, you have people that shed a bad light on everyone. Today's professional nanny is an educated woman with a genuine love of children who wouldn't want to do anything else."

 "Working nannies fight stereotypes," by Cesar G. Soriano, July 28, 2005.

Terminating a Nanny You've Been Happy With

If you're planning to let your nanny go for personal reasons—perhaps one of you will no longer be working, your child will be starting day care, or your priorities have changed in some other way—your timeline and approach should be completely different than when firing a nanny.

For starters, you should give the nanny ample advance notice, so that she can start looking for an alternate position. Approximately one to two months' notice is appropriate (unless you've signed an employment contract that states some other period of time).

Of course, you're risking her finding another job and leaving before you're ready. One way to forestall this is to offer her a bonus if she stays until the day your plans are changing. Another way to help control the situation is to ask among your friends, and see if you can find her another job before she starts looking! If you've been happy with your nanny, your friends will be delighted to hear about it, and you may find someone who's willing or able to match their schedule to yours.

In preparation for delivering the news to your nanny, draft a letter of recommendation that she can take with her when hunting for future jobs. Of course, you can make clear that potential employers can call you as well, but there's nothing like a written letter to make your nanny feel good and to impress other parents right up front.

As with any interaction, be businesslike, and cut to the chase quickly. Explain the change in your family situation and that you've been happy with her services, but wanted to give her plenty of time to find a new job.

Although she's not being fired, she may understandably feel shocked. Job change is never easy. Lay out everything you're willing to do to help her with that process. If you haven't already found job leads through your friends, you might ask whether she'd like you to place ads online and elsewhere, telling other parents that you have a great nanny whom you're trying to help find a new job and inviting them to contact you.

Some parents also give the nanny severance pay—for example, one week's pay for every year she has worked for you.

Also ask whether she's willing to sit down with you on another day for an exit interview. (Not today—she'll need a little time to collect her thoughts.) This is a good chance for both of you to reflect on your time together, and for her to offer tips on how you might make the situation more workable for the *next nanny*.

On the nanny's last day, consider giving her some meaningful gifts—perhaps some framed drawings by your children and a gift certificate for a massage or visit to a local spa. At a more practical level, if she hasn't found another job yet, remind her that she may be eligible for state unemployment compensation (assuming you've been paying her legally).

Avoiding Wrongful Termination Lawsuits

Although you don't have to come up with good cause before terminating a nanny (assuming you've employed her at will, as provided for in our sample employment agreement), legal limits do still apply to your right to fire her. You might have noticed that the contract provision itself states that you can't fire the nanny for any "illegal reason."

What types of reasons are illegal? Discrimination (either based on race or some other ground found in your state's law), violations of public policy, or retaliation against the nanny for complaining about on-the-job issues like an unsafe work environment or harassment might all qualify, depending on the laws in your state. A sufficiently disgruntled nanny might protest her firing by suing you for "wrongful termination," alleging that you fired her for a reason like one of these.

In fact, says attorney Bob King, "It's typically not during the hiring process when a nanny sues a family, but during the termination process. The hiring process is generally oblique—the rejected job candidates may have no idea why you decided not to hire them. But when a nanny says to a family, 'I'm pregnant,' and they say, 'You're fired,' the nanny immediately feels wronged and may pursue a wrongful termination suit. Here in California, for example, she'd have legal protection based on the pregnancy."

A nanny who has decided to sue may add a few other types of allegations besides wrongful termination into the mix, such as violations of wage and hour laws, sexual harassment, or various types of personal injuries, such as humiliation, defamation (in that your firing has hurt her chances of finding future employment), interference with prospective economic advantage, invasion of privacy, and intentional infliction of emotional distress. Again, the range of possibilities depends partly on your state's laws.

As long as you've dealt with your nanny fairly throughout her tenure, and are letting her go for a rational reason, you should be fine. But if you think the firing will anger your nanny enough to look for a reason to sue—or you have a sense that you're doing something that could be viewed as unfair—you might want to consult with a lawyer to make sure the law is on your side.

> **CONSULT A PRO**
> **Looking for an experienced lawyer?** Check out the in-depth information about lawyers across the United States found in Nolo's Lawyer Directory at www.nolo.com.

Given the ever-present risk of a lawsuit, you might be wondering whether your homeowner's or renter's insurance will protect you from lawsuits by your nanny. The short answer is no, this isn't part of the standard homeowner's or renter's policy. You might, however, be able to buy an endorsement to the policy that at least covers personal injury types of claims.

The typical umbrella policy won't help either. (An umbrella policy is meant to provide coverage for claims over and above what a basic policy covers.) The trouble is, coverage under most umbrella policies kicks in only when the claim merits some coverage under the primary policy. But there is a type of umbrella insurance that contains what's called a "drop-down" provision, which provides protection specifically for claims that the primary or underlying policy doesn't cover. Talk to your insurance broker (and, in particular, make sure that household employees don't fall within an exclusion under the umbrella policy).

If you're particularly risk averse, or have valuable assets to protect, you could purchase a separate employer's policy, called an "employment practices liability" policy. Most parents don't do so, but the costs of such coverage have apparently been coming down.

Index

Go to **Nolo.com/newsletters/index.html** to sign up for free newsletters and discounts on Nolo products.

- **Nolo Briefs.** Our monthly email newsletter with great deals and free information.

- **Nolo's Special Offer.** A monthly newsletter with the biggest Nolo discounts around.

- **BizBriefs.** Tips and discounts on Nolo products for business owners and managers.

- **Landlord's Quarterly.** Deals and free tips just for landlords and property managers, too.

 Don't forget to check for updates at **Nolo.com**. Under "Products," find this book and click "Legal Updates."

Let Us Hear From You

 Comments on this book? We want to hear 'em. Email us at feedback@nolo.com.

USHELP1

NOLO® *Online Legal Forms*

Nolo offers a large library of legal solutions and forms, created by Nolo's in-house legal staff. These reliable documents can be prepared in minutes.

Create a Document

- **Incorporation.** Incorporate your business in any state.
- **LLC Formations.** Gain asset protection and pass-through tax status in any state.
- **Wills.** Nolo has helped people make over 2 million wills. Is it time to make or revise yours?
- **Living Trust (avoid probate).** Plan now to save your family the cost, delays, and hassle of probate.
- **Trademark.** Protect the name of your business or product.
- **Provisional Patent.** Preserve your rights under patent law and claim "patent pending" status.

Download a Legal Form

Nolo.com has hundreds of top quality legal forms available for download—bills of sale, promissory notes, nondisclosure agreements, LLC operating agreements, corporate minutes, commercial lease and sublease, motor vehicle bill of sale, consignment agreements and many more.

Review Your Documents

Many lawyers in Nolo's consumer-friendly lawyer directory will review Nolo documents for a very reasonable fee. Check their detailed profiles at **Nolo.com/lawyers/index.html**.